DK EYEWI

TOP 10
VENICE

GILLIAN PRICE

Penguin
Random
House

Top 10 Venice Highlights

The Top 10 of Everything

CONTENTS

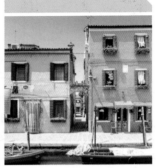

Venice
Area by Area

Streetsmart

The information in this DK Eyewitness Top 10 Travel Guide is checked regularly. Every effort has been made to ensure that this book is as up to date as possible at the time of going to press. Some details, however, such as telephone numbers, opening hours, prices, gallery hanging arrangements and travel information are liable to change. The publishers cannot accept responsibility for any consequences arising from the use of this book, nor for any material on third-party websites, and cannot guarantee that any website address in this book will be a suitable source of travel information. We value the views and suggestions of our readers very highly. Please write to: Publisher, DK Eyewitness Travel Guides, Dorling Kindersley, 80 Strand, London WC2R 0RL, UK, or email travelguides@dk.com

Within each Top 10 list in this book, no hierarchy of quality or popularity is implied. All 10 are, in the editor's opinion, of roughly equal merit.

Front cover and spine *Gondolas moored on the Grand Canal at San Marco*
Back cover *Crowds enjoying San Marco during the summertime*
Title page *Basilica di Santa Maria della Salute on the Grand Canal*

Welcome to
Venice

Gliding gondolas. Glorious sunsets over the lagoon. Spritz *aperitivos*. Black cuttlefish-ink pasta. Renaissance *palazzi*. Gorgeous Carnival masks. A time warp. And no cars; not one. It doesn't matter how many times you've been, a visit to Venice is always as memorable as it is romantic. Navigating the canal-filled city is easy with this Eyewitness Top 10 Venice guide.

There's nothing like Venice anywhere else in the world. You can join the crowds thronging **Piazza San Marco** and wonder at the glittering **Basilica**. Relax at the outdoor cafés, drinking in the atmosphere along with a cappuccino, or ride a water-bus plying the canals.

Whether you come for a couple of days or a whole week, our *Top 10 Venice* guide is invaluable, with its carefully selected listings that bring together the best the city has to offer. Explore the labyrinthine **Doge's Palace**, have a drink in buzzing **Campo Santa Margherita**, hunt for a costume for the annual **Carnival** bash, shop at top craft stores and fashion boutiques, or travel to the atmospheric islands of **Murano** and **Torcello**.

Succinct descriptions explain how Venice developed as and where it did, with the help of stars such as Marco Polo and Vivaldi. Insider tips abound, along with curious facts and figures that you won't find in any other guide. Your questions will be answered: Is Venice still sinking? Do people often fall in the water?

Whether you're coming for a weekend or a week, our Top 10 guide brings together the best of everything the city can offer. There are tips throughout, from seeking out what's free to avoiding the crowds, plus ten easy-to-follow itineraries, designed to help you visit a clutch of sights in a short space of time. Add inspiring photography and detailed maps, and you've got the essential pocket-sized travel companion. **Enjoy the book, and enjoy Venice.**

Clockwise from top: Giudecca; lion statue in Piazza San Marco; Basilica San Marco mosaic; Grand Canal; Carnival mask; gondolas with San Giorgio Maggiore in the background; Burano

Exploring Venice

Venice is a sightseeing paradise for people of all ages. To make the most of a holiday and see the best the city has to offer, here are some time-efficient ideas for both two- and four-day stays.

The Grand Canal cuts a meandering path through Venice and offers a delightful perspective from the water.

Two Days in Venice

Day ❶
MORNING
Start off at the marvellous **Basilica** (see pp12–15) before a wander around the **Piazza San Marco** (see pp20–21). The Campanile tower gives a superb view over the city.
AFTERNOON
A visit to the **Doge's Palace** (see pp16–19) can be followed by a laid-back ride on a *vaporetto* all the way up the glorious **Grand Canal** (see pp24–5) past many elegant *palazzi* and under the Accademia and Rialto bridges.

Day ❷
MORNING
Begin with Venetian art at the **Accademia Galleries** (see pp30–31) before strolling through to **Campo Santa Margherita** (see pp38–9) for a bite to eat.
AFTERNOON
It's a short walk to the Venetian Gothic masterpiece **Santa Maria Gloriosa dei Frari** (see pp32–3) and, from there, on to **Campo San Polo** (see p89) with its great neighbourhood feel.

Four Days in Venice

Day ❶
MORNING
The natural place to start any visit is the magnificent main square, **Piazza San Marco** (see pp20–21). A visit to the panoramic Campanile or the Torre dell'Orologio (booking essential) can be followed by a coffee at the legendary – but expensive – **Caffè Florian** (see p21). Refreshed, head into the **Basilica** (see pp12–15) to wonder at the ancient mosaics.
AFTERNOON
After lunch, take time to explore the **Doge's Palace** (see pp16–19), once the powerhouse of the Maritime Republic. Don't miss the Bridge of Sighs and the dank prisons.

The impressive Doge's Palace dominates the waterfront leading to Piazza San Marco

The island of Burano is well worth a visit for its splendid array of colourful houses.

Day ❷
MORNING
Catch a *vaporetto* at Piazzale Roma or the railway station for the spectacular trip along the **Grand Canal** *(see p24–5)*, passing beneath Rialto Bridge. Alight at Salute to visit the **Punta della Dogana** *(see p98)*.

AFTERNOON
After lunch on the sun-blessed **Zattere** *(see p101)*, backtrack to see the impressive **Peggy Guggenheim Collection** *(see pp40–41)*.

Day ❸
MORNING
Make an early start to enjoy the best of the Rialto fish and produce market, which is open mostly in the morning *(see pp34–5)*. It's then just a short walk to the church of **Santa Maria Gloriosa dei Frari** *(see pp32–3)*, a masterpiece of Venetian Gothic architecture.

AFTERNOON
Campo Santa Margherita *(see pp38–9)* is a bustling square with inviting cafés and restaurants ideal for lunch. After you have eaten, proceed to the **Accademia Galleries** *(see pp30–31)* for an overview of Venetian painting through the centuries.

Day ❹
MORNING
Take a leisurely ferry trip over the Northern Lagoon to the island of **Torcello** *(see pp36–7)*, where you can admire the Byzantine mosaics in the Basilica. Then continue to neighbouring **Burano** *(see p121)* or **Mazzorbo** *(see p117)* for lunch.

AFTERNOON
Pick up a ferry to take you cruising via Treporti and **Punta Sabbioni** to the **Lido** *(see pp123–4)* for a trip to the beach. Afterwards, head back to Venice proper.

Top 10 Venice Highlights

Basilica di Santa Maria della Salute
viewed from Ponte dell'Accademia

TOP10 Venice Highlights

The uniquely romantic city of Venice was built entirely on water and has managed to survive into the 21st century without cars. Narrow alleyways and canals pass between sumptuous palaces and magnificent churches, colourful neighbourhood markets and quiet backwaters, unchanged for centuries. Few cities possess such an awesome line-up of sights for visitors.

Basilica San Marco **1**

Venice's fairy-tale cathedral is distinctly Byzantine, and its façade and interior have been embellished with resplendent mosaics and works of art through the ages (see pp12–15).

2 Doge's Palace

This was the powerhouse of the city's rulers for nearly 900 years. Passing through the maze of gilded rooms gives visitors a fascinating insight into the extravagant lifestyle that so often accompanied state affairs (see pp16–19).

3 Piazza San Marco

Elegance and opulence sit side by side in what Napoleon named "the finest drawing room in Europe". This magnificent square is adorned with monuments that bear testimony to Venice's history (see pp20–23).

4 Grand Canal

The city's majestic watercourse swarms with all manner of boats, while its embankments boast a dazzling succession of palaces dating back as early as the 13th century (see pp24–7).

5. Accademia Galleries
An unsurpassed collection of Venetian paintings, with masterpieces by Titian, Bellini and Giorgione. A must, not only for art lovers *(see pp30–31).*

Santa Maria Gloriosa dei Frari 6
A Gothic interior with grandiose works of art lies in store behind this church's brick façade *(see pp32–3).*

7. The Rialto
A fresh produce market has enlivened this quayside since medieval times and is arguably still the best market in the world *(see pp34–5).*

8. Torcello
Escape the crowds in the city with a ferry ride over the vast expanse of the lagoon to this peaceful, lush island, the site of Venice's original settlement *(see pp36–7).*

Campo Santa Margherita 9
A wonderful square, always bustling with life thanks to its market stalls and outdoor cafés. An added bonus are the many architectural styles *(see pp38–9).*

10. Peggy Guggenheim Collection
Italy's leading museum for 20th-century European and American art. The collection is housed in a palace on the Grand Canal *(see pp40–41).*

metres 300
yards 300

TOP 10 ⭐ Basilica San Marco

The breathtaking Byzantine basilica dominating Piazza San Marco *(see pp20–23)* was constructed in such ornate fashion for two reasons: as an embodiment of the Venetian Republic's power and as a fitting resting place for St Mark. Serving as the doges' chapel, it was the site of coronations, funerals and processions, all gloriously framed by more than 4,000 sq m (43,000 sq ft) of mosaics, eastern treasures and 500 columns, some dating back to the 3rd century.

Western Façade ①
A marvellous succession of domes, columns, arches and spires, **(right)** interspersed with marble statues, screens and glittering mosaics, greets tourists in Piazza San Marco. The northernmost arch houses 13th-century mosaics that depict the basilica itself. Other mosaics are 17th- and 18th-century copies.

② Atrium Mosaics
These glorious mosaics **(left)** of precious gold-leaf over glass tiles were created in the Byzantine tradition by expert craftsmen, and give detailed accounts of the Old Testament. The 13th-century cupola's concentric circles recount 24 episodes from Genesis, including the Creation and Adam and Eve.

③ Flooring
The elaborate paving is a mosaic masterpiece of multicoloured stones on uneven levels, evocative of the sea. Intricate geometrical designs sit alongside animal shapes.

Basilica Floorplan

Pala d'Oro ④
The dazzling jewel-encrusted gold screen **(right)** was commissioned in Constantinople in 976 but frequently added to at later dates. It boasts 250 panels bearing 1,927 authentic gems and cloisonné plaques.

BUILDING THE BASILICA

Construction began on the first building in 829. However, during a revolt in 976, it was burned down and dismantled. The current building, a Greek cross layout surmounted by five domes, dates from 1071. The main architect is shown over the central portal, biting his fingers in frustration over a building defect. The basilica became the city cathedral in 1807.

Ascension Dome

The central dome has a spectacular array of early 13th-century mosaics, depicting the New Testament. *Christ in Glory* is shown above depictions of the Virtues **(right)**.

8 Pentecost Dome

Probably the first dome of the basilica to be adorned with mosaics, it is illustrated with the Descent of the Holy Ghost, seen as a flame over the heads of the 12 apostles.

9 Basilica Museum

Here you'll find the famed quartet of horses crafted from bronze and covered in gold. Booty from the Fourth Crusade, these restored Graeco-Roman equine figures originally graced the Hippodrome in Constantinople.

Loggia dei Cavalli 10

Replicas of the proud horses, now in the museum, stand on this balcony overlooking Piazza San Marco **(right)**. Visitors can also see clutches of columns, whose dimensions and decorative styles indicate their origins.

The Tetrarchs 5

The inspiration for these red porphyry rock figures is unknown. They probably represent the four emperors of the eastern and western Roman empires **(right)**. The statue was pillaged from Constantinople during the Fourth Crusade in 1204.

6 Treasury

The basilica's glittering riches include precious chalices of rock crystal enamelled by medieval silver- and goldsmiths and reliquaries from Venice's eastern conquests, including parts of the True Cross.

NEED TO KNOW

MAP Q5 ▪ Piazza San Marco ▪ 041 270 83 11 ▪ www.basilicasanmarco.it ▪ No disabled access beyond ground floor ▪ Guided visits – book on www.alata.it ▪ Bookshop

Basilica: Open Easter–Oct: 9:45am–5pm Mon–Sat, 2–5pm Sun & pub hols; Nov–Easter: 9:45am–5pm Mon–Sat, 2–4pm Sun & pub hols

Pala d'Oro, treasury and Loggia dei Cavalli: Open Easter–Oct: same as basilica; Nov–Easter: 9:45am–4pm Mon–Sat, 2–4pm Sun & pub hols. Admission: Pala d'Oro €2; treasury €3

Museum: Open 9:45am–4:45pm daily all year. Admission: €5

▪ Visit at dusk, when the setting sun lights up the façade.

▪ Take binoculars to examine the mosaics, but you must leave backpacks in the luggage room.

Basilica Architectural Features

 Galleries
The airy catwalks over the body of the basilica reflect the eastern tradition of segregation in worship, as they were exclusively for women. They are closed to visitors.

 Stone Wall-Slabs
Brick-faced until the 1100s, the walls were then covered with stone slabs from the East, sliced lengthways to produce a kaleidoscopic effect.

3 **Romanesque Stone Carvings**
The exquisite semicircular stone carvings over the central doorway were executed between 1235 and 1265 and still bear traces of their original colouring.

4 **The "Victory Bringer"**
This revered Byzantine icon is given pride of place in the Madonna of Nicopeia Chapel. Rumoured to have been executed by St Luke, it was carried into battle for its miraculous powers.

5 **Baptistry**
Aglow with 14th-century mosaic scenes of the life of St John, this is also home to the tomb of Italian architect Jacopo Sansovino (see p49). Open for prayer only.

Basilica Floorplan

Font in the Baptistry

6 **Zen Chapel**
The ornate decoration in this chapel was executed for the funeral of its namesake, Cardinal Zen, in 1521, in recognition of his gifts to the state. Open for prayer only.

The ornate Iconostasis

7 **Iconostasis**
This elaborate screen separates the worship area of the chancel from the nave. Atop its eight columns are Gothic-style statues of the Virgin and the apostles, sculpted by the Dalle Masegne brothers in 1394.

8 **Byzantine Pierced Screens**
Influenced by eastern architecture, delicate geometrical designs and lattice-work stone screens are featured on all three façades, in the atrium and loggia.

9 **Porta dei Fiori**
This doorway on the northern façade bears a 13th-century nativity scene surrounded by Moorish arches.

10 **Altar Columns**
Four finely carved alabaster and marble columns support a canopy at the altar, beneath which lies the body of St Mark.

ST MARK, PATRON SAINT OF VENICE

Although the well-loved saint of Byzantium, St Theodore, had been appointed protector of Venice by the Byzantine emperor, the fledgling republic felt in need of a saint of its own. According to legend, in AD 828, two adroit Venetian merchants filched the body of St Mark from a monastery in Alexandria, transporting it under layers of pork fat to conceal it from Muslim guards. The welcome in Venice was triumphant, and the story was recounted in countless paintings and mosaics. The remains, however, were mislaid for years, until an arm miraculously broke through a column in 1094 (marked by a small cross, left of the Altar of the Sacrament) in answer to a prayer. St Mark now rests in peace beneath the basilica's main altar. The ubiquitous winged lion representing St Mark could be found throughout the republic as the trademark of Venetian dominion: it is

often shown with two paws in the sea and two on land, to symbolize the geography of Venice.

The Miracle of the Relic of the True Cross on the Rialto Bridge (1494) by Vittore Carpaccio

TOP 10
VENICE RELICS

1 Milk of the Virgin Mary, Basilica Treasury *(see p13)*

2 Blood of Christ, Basilica Treasury

3 Nail from the True Cross, Chiesa di San Pantalon *(see p53)*

4 Thorn from Christ's crown, Basilica Treasury

5 Body of St Mark, Basilica San Marco *(see pp12–13)*

6 Body of St Lucy, Chiesa di San Geremia

7 Three rocks used to stone St Stephen to death, Basilica Treasury

8 Skull of St John the Baptist, Basilica Treasury

9 Leg of St George, Basilica Treasury

10 Foot of St Catherine of Siena, Santi Giovanni e Paolo *(see p52)*

This mosaic in Basilica San Marco depicts the veneration of the body of St Mark by the Doge.

🔟 ⭐ Doge's Palace

A magnificent combination of Byzantine, Gothic and Renaissance architecture, the Palazzo Ducale (Doge's Palace) was the official residence of the 120 doges who ruled Venice from 697 to 1797. A fortress-like structure stood here in the 9th century, to be replaced by the elegant Gothic version seen today, despite a string of fires in the 1500s. Artists such as Titian, Tintoretto and Bellini vied with each other to embellish the palace with painting and sculpture, not to mention architects Antonio Rizzo and Pietro Lombardo, the latter responsible for the western façade.

1 Façade
Elegant twin façades face the piazzetta and the quayside. Pink-and-cream stonework and a loggia stand above an arcade of columns with 36 sculpted Istrian stone capitals **(above)**.

2 Sala del Senato
Senate members met in this lavish hall **(below)** to debate war, foreign affairs and trade with the Doge. Time was measured by two clocks – one with a 24-hour face, the other with zodiac signs.

3 Armoury
A fascinating, if spine-chilling, collection of beautifully crafted firearms, ceremonial weapons and suits of armour **(left)** from Asia and the West. Among the war trophies is a Turkish standard brought back from the Battle of Lepanto (1571).

4 Prisons
A fascinating maze of cells is linked by corridors and staircases on both sides of the canal. One of the most famous inmates, Casanova *(see p44)*, made a dramatic escape across the roof in 1756. The "new prisons" were in use until the 1940s and feature poignant graffiti by internees.

Scala d'Oro ⑦

The magnificent Golden Staircase **(right)**, so-called for its Classical stucco decorations in 24-carat gold-leaf framing frescoes, led guests of honour to the second floor. Designed by Sansovino *(see p49)*, it was later completed by Scarpagnino in 1559.

⑤ Bridge of Sighs

One of the world's most famous bridges **(above)**, the Ponte dei Sospiri is an early 17th-century Baroque structure that crosses to the palace prisons. It reputedly caused the condemned to "sigh" at their last glimpse of sky and sea.

⑥ Sala dello Scudo

Enormous globes **(below)** and painted wall maps showing the known world in 1762 make this room a must. The map of Eastern Asia traces Marco Polo's travels to China, complete with camels, rhinos and the mythical Uncharted Lands of the People Eaters.

⑧ Porta della Carta

The palace's main entrance (now the visitors' exit) has a beautifully sculpted 1438 portal by the Bon family. The name "paper door" arose because edicts were posted here.

⑨ Sala del Maggior Consiglio

The Great Council Chamber **(left)** is lined with canvases of Venetian victories and a cornice frieze of 76 doges – a black curtain represents traitor Marin Falier *(see p19)*.

⑩ Doge's Apartments

The communicating rooms of the Doge's living quarters include rich brocades, triumphal friezes, gilded ceilings and works of art.

Doge's Palace Art and Architecture

Veronese's *Rape of Europa*

1 Rape of Europa
Veronese's allegorical work (1580) in the AntiCollegio shows Europa sitting on a bull, alias Jove, who is nuzzling her foot.

2 Paradise
Possibly the world's largest oil painting (1588–90), by Jacopo and Domenico Tintoretto, it is said to contain 800 figures (Sala del Maggior Consiglio).

3 Arcade Capital
Proclaimed the "most beautiful in Europe" by art critic John Ruskin, this eight-sided carved capital on the southwest corner shows the zodiac signs and planets in imaginative detail.

4 The Triumph of Venice
Dominating the Sala del Senato is Tintoretto's glorious work of propaganda (1580–84), showing allegorical and mythological figures proffering fruits of the sea to Venice.

5 Central Balcony
This magnificent early 15th-century stone terrace, embellished with columns, spires and a host of saints, opens off the Sala del Maggior Consiglio with a breathtaking view of the lagoon.

6 Arco Foscari
This triumphal archway of pink-and-cream stone layers leading to the Giants' Staircase was commissioned by Doge Foscari in 1438.

7 Wellheads
Elaborate 16th-century wellheads were constructed to drain water from the gutters to the palace's central courtyard.

8 Drunkenness of Noah
A powerful sculpture from the early 15th century adorns the façade's southeast corner. Noah, inebriated and half-naked before his sons, is intended to portray the weakness of man.

Drunkenness of Noah

9 Coronation of the Virgin
The faded but inspired remains of Guariento's fresco, discovered beneath Tintoretto's *Paradise*, are housed in a side room, with panels explaining the restoration techniques.

10 Giants' Staircase
So named for its two colossal statues of Mars and Neptune, which were sculpted by Sansovino in 1567 as symbols of Venice's power. Visiting dignitaries would ascend the marble-lined stairs to the palace.

Giants' Staircase

THE EXTENT OF THE VENETIAN REPUBLIC

Doge Gradenigo with the Venetian fleet at the siege of Chioggia, 1379

In its earliest days, Venice was little more than a huddle of islands in the middle of a shallow marshy lagoon, settled by a band of refugees from the Veneto region. Yet over the centuries it developed into a mighty republic reaching south to the Mediterranean and north to the Alps, based on the concept of trade. Salt was stored in massive warehouses, there were dealings in exotic spices and wondrous fabrics from the East, crusades were organized and fitted out here, and relics procured. Its main population probably never exceeded 160,000, however, well beyond its walled port towns, which stretched down the Dalmatian coast, were far-flung outposts such as Crete and Cyprus. These dominions protected key passages in commerce with the Arabic countries. Westward across the Po plain, Venice's influence took in Treviso, Vicenza and Verona, extending all the way to Bergamo on the outskirts of Milan and the mighty Visconti dynasty.

The Republic's gaining of maritime power is celebrated in *The Victorious Return of Doge Andrea Contarini after Triumph in Chioggia* by Paolo Veronese (1525–88).

TOP 10
EVENTS IN THE VENETIAN REPUBLIC

1 Venice founded on 25 April (St Mark's Day, AD 421)

2 First doge, Paoluccio Anafesto, elected (697)

3 St Mark's body brought to Venice (828)

4 Ruthless siege of Constantinople during the Fourth Crusade under Doge Enrico Dandolo (1204)

5 Venice loses 60 per cent of its population to the Black Death (1348)

6 Doge Marin Falier decapitated for conspiracy (1355)

7 Genoese defeated at Battle of Chioggia, leaving Venice to reign over the Adriatic and Mediterranean (1381)

8 Victory over Turks at Battle of Lepanto (1571)

9 After 25 years of war, Crete is lost to the Turks (1669)

10 Napoleon invades the Veneto, bringing about the fall of the Venetian Republic (1797)

🔟 ⭐ Piazza San Marco

Long the political and religious heart of Venice, it's hard to believe Piazza San Marco was once just a monastery garden crossed by a stream. The glittering basilica and Doge's Palace command the east side of the square, while other stately buildings along its borders have been the backdrop for magnificent processions. The western end was remodelled by Napoleon, who wished to construct a royal palace here. Today the piazza continues to bustle, with a museum complex *(see p22)*, cafés and costumed Carnival crowds.

1 **Basilica San Marco**
See pp12–15.

2 **Doge's Palace**
See pp16–19.

3 **Torre dell'Orologio**

A marvel to behold, the imposing and impressive Renaissance-style clock tower is topped by two bronze Moors **(left)** hammering out the hours on the upper terrace. At Epiphany and Ascension there is an hourly procession of clockwork Magi that are led by an angel. According to legend, the craftsmen were subsequently blinded to prevent them repeating the work.

The Piazzetta and the Palace

NEED TO KNOW

MAP Q5

Campanile: Open Easter–Oct: 9am–7pm daily (Jul–Sep: 9am–9pm); Nov–Easter: 9:30am–3:45pm daily. Admission €8

Torre dell'Orologio: 041 271 59 11; Open 10am & 11am Mon–Wed, 2pm & 3pm Thu–Sun. Admission €12. No disabled access

Museo Correr Complex: Open 10am–7pm (Nov–Mar: 10am–5pm). Admission €16 (includes Doge's Palace)

■ The best time to appreciate the beauty of the square is early morning, when only the city sweepers are here.

Campanile **4**
Incomparable views of the city and lagoon can be had by taking the elevator to the top of this 98-m (323-ft) bell tower **(right)**. It was masterfully rebuilt to its 16th-century design following its clamorous collapse in 1902.

5 **Piazzetta**
Once an inlet for boats and witness to the arrival of distinguished visitors during the Republic's heyday, this now fully paved mini square fronts the lagoon.

6 Column of San Marco

This is one of two granite columns erected in 1172 by Nicolò Barattieri **(left)**; the other symbolizes San Teodoro. Public executions were held here.

Plan of Piazza San Marco

VENICE'S BELLS

Booming through the city, the five bells in the Campanile have been employed to mark Venice's rhythms for centuries. The Maleficio bell was sounded to announce an execution, the Nona rang at midday, the Trottiera spurred on the nobles' horses for assemblies in the Doge's Palace and the Mezza Terza was used to indicate that the Senate was in session. The Marangona bell is still sounded to mark midnight.

7 Procuratie Vecchie and Nuove

The Procurators, who were responsible for state administration, lived in these elegant 15th-century buildings **(below)**.

8 Piazzetta dei Leoncini

This is the site of a former vegetable market, where a pair of small lions *(leoncini)* carved from red Verona stone **(right)** have been crouching since 1722.

9 Caffè Florian

Reputedly Europe's first coffee house, the premises still retain their original 1720 wood-panelling, marble-topped tables and gilt-framed mirrors *(see p83)*.

10 Giardinetti Reali

These shady public gardens, created during the Napoleonic era, took the place of boatyards and grain stores, situated just behind the panoramic waterfront.

Museo Correr Complex

1 Biblioteca Marciana Ceiling
The ceiling vault of the opulent reading room (sale monumentali), inside the Libreria Sansoviniana, collapsed in 1545 and architect Sansovino imprisoned – he was released to complete the job at his own expense. Titian selected artists for the decorations; Veronese was awarded a gold chain for the best work.

2 Libreria Sansoviniana Staircase
Bedecked with gilt and stucco decorations by Alessandro Vittoria, the 16th-century stair-case leads from a monumental entrance on the piazza to the halls of the old library.

Canova's statue of Orpheus

3 Veneziano Paintings
This prolific Byzantine artist is featured in the Pinacoteca's Room 25 (part of Museo Correr), with glowing two-dimensional religious portraits (1290–1302).

Correr Ballroom

4 Correr Ballroom
This showy Neo-Classical creation was built for Napoleon. It is now used for exhibitions.

5 Two Venetian Ladies
Carpaccio's masterpiece of well-dressed ladies (1500–10) is in Room 38 of the Museo Correr. It was first thought to depict courtesans, but the women are, in fact, awaiting their menfolk's return from hunting.

6 Canova Statues
In the Museo Correr, works by Antonio Canova (1767–1822), foremost sculptor of his time, include his acclaimed statues of Orpheus and Eurydice.

7 Map of Venice
Pride of place in Room 32 of the Museo Correr goes to Jacopo de' Barbari's prospective map-layout of Venice (1497–1500), which was painstakingly engraved on six pear-wood panels.

8 Bellini Room
Works by the talented Bellini family are on display in Room 36 of the Pinacoteca: the poignant *Dead Christ Supported by Two Angels* (1453–5) by the best known, Giovanni; head of the family Jacopo's *Crucifixion* (1450); and son Gentile's portrait of *Doge Giovanni Mocenigo* (1475).

9 Narwhal Tusk
Once prized as the horn of the fabled unicorn, this 1.6-m- (5-ft-) long tusk from the rare whale has been superbly carved with Jesse's and Jesus's family tree (Room 40 in Museo Correr).

10 Crafts and Guilds
Wooden sandals 60-cm (24-inches) high, inlaid with mother-of-pearl, illustrate the stiff demands put upon followers of 15th–17th-century fashion (Room 48).

ACQUA ALTA FLOODING

Acqua Alta ("high water") has long been disruptive to the city between October and March. As warning sirens fill the air, people drag out their waterproof boots, shopkeepers rush to put up protective barriers and street-sweepers lay out duck-boards in low-lying spots. Venice and its lagoon are subject to the tides of the Adriatic Sea but flood levels are caused by the coincidence of low atmospheric pressure, strong sirocco winds from the south and natural high tides due to moon phases. Piazza San Marco is among the most vulnerable spots. The flood gates designed for the Lido sea entrances are held by many experts to be both useless and harmful to the lagoon. However, there are plans for an elaborate drainage system on the piazza, dredging canals and raising paving levels.

Bullfight in St Mark's Square by Canaletto and Giovanni Battista Cimaroli

Piazza San Marco is located in a vulnerable position on the edge of the lagoon and has been flooded by high tides throughout its history.

TOP 10
HISTORIC EVENTS IN PIAZZA SAN MARCO

1 Foundations of Doge's Palace laid (AD 814)

2 Construction of basilica started (828)

3 First bullfight held (1162)

4 Square paved with brick, herringbone-style (1267)

5 Square paved with volcanic trachyte blocks (1722–35)

6 Napoleon demolishes San Geminiano church to make way for Ala Napoleonica (1810)

7 Campanile crumbles to the ground (1902)

8 Record flood 1.94 m (6.4 ft) above sea level (4 November 1966)

9 Pink Floyd rock concert attracts 100,000 (1989)

10 Campanile stormed by separatists (1997)

TOP 10 ⭐ Grand Canal

Venice's majestic "highway", the Canal Grande, is only one of the 177 canals flowing through the city, but at some 4 km (2.5 miles) in length, 30–70 m (98–230 ft) in width and averaging 4.5 m (15 ft) in depth, it certainly earns its name. Snaking its way through the city with a double curve, its banks are lined with exquisite palaces, while on its waters colourful flotillas of gondolas, ferries, taxi launches, high-speed police boats and barges groaning under loads of fresh produce provide endless fascination. In 1818, when the water was cleaner, Lord Byron swam all the way down the Grand Canal from the Lido.

① Fondaco dei Turchi
With an exotic air and its round arches, this Veneto-Byzantine building (1225) **(above)** was the Turkish trade centre for 200 years. It is now the Natural History Museum *(see p60)*.

② Ca' Pesaro
This colossal Baroque palace, decorated with diamond-point ashlar work, was the final creation of architect Longhena. Home to the city's modern art collections, it is beautifully floodlit at night *(see p55)*.

The view towards Santa Maria della Salute

③ Rialto Bridge
One of the city's most familiar sights, the striking 28-m- (92-ft-) wide, 8-m- (26-ft-) high Istrian stone Ponte di Rialto **(below)** dates from 1588.

④ Riva del Vin
A sunny quayside with a string of open-air restaurants, this is one of the few accessible banks of the Grand Canal. Barrels of wine *(vino)* used to be off-loaded here, hence the name.

⑤ Ca' Rezzonico
The finest feature of this imposing palace is its grandiose staircase **(right)**. Today it is a museum of 18th-century Venice.

7 Ca' Dario

With an ornamental Renaissance façade studded with multicoloured stone medallions, this lopsided palace is supposedly cursed due to a number of misfortunes that have overtaken its various owners.

6 Accademia Bridge

The lovely wooden Ponte dell'Accademia **(above)**, built in 1932 by the engineer Miozzi, was intended as a temporary measure until a more substantial structure was designed, but it is now a permanent fixture. It affords stunning views of the Grand Canal.

8 Santa Maria della Salute

Longhena's 17th-century masterpiece of sculpted whorls beneath a towering dome **(right)**, this church commemorates the end of a devastating plague in the city *(see p52)*.

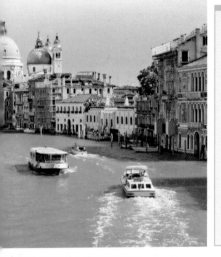

WAVE DAMAGE

Damage to buildings caused by wash has worsened of late with the rise in motor-propelled craft. Waves provoked by all boats eat into foundations of buildings on the water's edge, as well as making life harder for the gondoliers. Speed limits aim to curb this: 7 kmph (4.5 mph) for private craft and 11 kmph (7 mph) for waterbuses on the Grand Canal. Narrower canals mean 5 kmph (3 mph), while 20 kmph (12.5 mph) is the lagoon maximum.

NEED TO KNOW

The Grand Canal runs from Piazzale Roma, the bus terminal and car park area, to Piazza San Marco. It is easily navigable courtesy of ferries Nos. 1 (all stops) and 2 (main stops only)

▪ Grab the front seats on *vaporetto* line No. 1 for the best views of the sights along the canal.

▪ To beat the crowds, start out from Piazzale Roma heading towards San Marco in the late afternoon or evening, or take the reverse direction in the morning.

9 Punta della Dogana

The figure of Fortune **(right)** stands atop the erstwhile customs house, now an arts centre *(see p98)*, and doubles as a weather vane. This is where the Grand Canal joins St Mark's Basin.

10 Harry's Bar

The legendary watering hole of Ernest Hemingway is where the Bellini *aperitivo* was invented *(see p67)*. Opened in 1931 by Arrigo Cipriani, it was named after the American who funded it.

Watercraft of Venice

Typical Venetian gondola

1 Gondola

These are most often seen transporting tourists around the canals. A larger version *(traghetto)* is also used for the cross-canal ferry *(see p139)*, while the smaller *gondolino* is a slender racing craft.

2 Vaporetto

Strictly speaking, this is the capacious rounded waterbus, now also seen in an "ecological" electric model. A slimmer *motoscafo* serves the outer runs and narrow canals with relatively low bridges.

3 Sandolo

A slim, lightweight boat perfectly suited to hunting and fishing in the shallow waters of the lagoon, not to mention racing. Painted black, these "imitation gondolas" can deceive tourists on the back canals.

4 Topo

The most common barge for transporting goods around the canals, it can be seen loaded with everything from washing machines to demijohns, often with a live dog "figurehead" on the prow.

5 Sanpierota

This flat-bottomed rowing boat is named after the inhabitants of San Pietro in Volta in the southern lagoon *(see p125)*. Once used for transporting fish to Venice, nowadays it is fitted with an outboard motor and photogenic oblique sail.

6 Bragozzo

With its gently rounded prow and stern, this brightly coloured sailing boat was traditionally used for fishing by the inhabitants of Chioggia *(see p125)*.

7 Fire Boat

From their station near Ca' Foscari, the red launches are called both to deal with fires and to rescue submerged obstacles and crumbling façades.

8 Garbage Vessel

The city's hefty waste-collecting AMAV barges trundle over the lagoon with the day's rubbish, in addition to carrying out environmental monitoring.

Ambulance launch

9 Ambulance and Police Launches

These modern craft attract plenty of attention as they roar down the canals – only the emergency categories are allowed to disregard the city's speed limits.

10 Car Ferry

These giants convey all manner of motor vehicles from the Tronchetto to the Lido.

VENICE'S GONDOLAS

The quintessential sleek Venetian gondola has been plying the city's canals since as early as the 11th century, although it did not take on its present graceful form until the late 1400s. Compared to a mere 405 gondolas on the waterways today, as many as 10,000 were in use in the late 19th century: bridges were once few and far between and gondolas acted as ferries between one island and another, a custom that continues to this day across the Grand Canal by the *traghetti*. A handful of gondola yards still construct the boats as well as carry out repairs, such as San Trovaso in Dorsoduro *(see p98)*. It's a costly and complex craft – eight different types of wood are needed for a total of 280 pieces to make the asymmetrical craft, 11 m (36 ft) in length and 1.42 m (4.5 ft) in width, at a cost approaching €25,000.

TOP 10
GONDOLA FEATURES

1 *Forcola* (rowlock)

2 *Ferro* (prow bracket)

3 *Hippocampus* (side ornament)

4 Night lamp

5 Bronze stern decoration

6 Ribbed oar

7 *Felze* (cabin)

8 Gondolier's foot rest

9 Gondolier's striped shirt

10 Gondolier's straw hat

The iron bracket (ferro) on the prow weighs 30 kg (66 lb) to offset the weight of the rower, and adds to the more than 350-kg (770-lb) weight of the gondola. Originally painted in bright colours, the black gondolas that you see today were decreed by the Senate to prevent excessive shows of wealth.

Gondola repair yard

TOP 10 ⭐ Accademia Galleries

A dazzling collection of masterpieces spanning the full development of Venetian art from Byzantine to Renaissance, Baroque and Rococo, the Gallerie dell'Accademia is Venice's equivalent of the Uffizi in Florence. Giovanni Battista Piazzetta started the collection in 1750 to serve as models for the art school; in 1807 it was boosted by Napoleon with the addition of works from suppressed churches. The same year the collection moved to its present premises, occupying three former religious establishments: the 12th–15th-century Scuola Grande di Santa Maria della Carità and its adjoining church, and a 12th-century monastery remodelled by Palladio in the 1500s. In the 1940s, architect Carlo Scarpa modernized the interior spaces *(see p49)*.

San Giobbe Altarpiece ❶

Giovanni Bellini's inspirational altarpiece **(right)** (Room 2) was painted in 1487 for the Church of San Giobbe. It is regarded as one of the finest examples of Sacra Conversazione, which was central to 15th-century Venetian art. The presence of St Sebastian and St Giobbe beside the Virgin suggests the aftermath of plague, while angel musicians pay homage to San Giobbe, patron saint of music.

❷ The Tempest

This enigmatic 1506 portrayal of a woman suckling her child **(left)** is by

Giorgione (Room 23). The overall impression is of the figures and the dream-like, stormy landscape blended into one whole.

❸ Supper in the House of Levi

The forceful canvas by Veronese (1573) occupies an entire wall of Room 10 and caused controversy in its time. The church authorities, who commissioned it as "The Last Supper", were angered by the inclusion of "dogs, buffoons, drunken Germans, dwarfs and other such absurdities" – so Veronese changed the title.

❹ Pietà

Titian's last work (1576) is unfinished but it is also considered his best (Room 10), imbued as it is with golden light and a piercing sense of anguish.

***Previous pages** Gondolas on the Grand Canal*

5 Meeting and Departure of the Betrothed Ursula and Ereo

Part of Carpaccio's magnificent narrative cycle (1495) about a Breton princess and an English prince can be seen in Room 21.

Gallery Floorplan

6 Procession in St Mark's Square

Part of Gentile Bellini's spectacular cycle (1496) of the St Mark's Day procession in 1444 **(above)** can be seen in Room 20.

7 Madonna dell'Arancio

This exquisite work (1496–8) by Cima da Conegliano, painted for a Murano Franciscan church, is enlivened with partridges and plant life (Room 2).

NEED TO KNOW

MAP L6 ■ Campo della Carità, Dorsoduro 1050 ■ 041 520 03 45 ■ www.gallerie accademia.org

Open 8:15am–7:15pm daily (2pm Mon; last admission 45 minutes before closing); closed 1 Jan, 1 May, 25 Dec

Admission €9

■ The galleries are currently undergoing extensive expansion, so the floorplan may differ from that shown here until the work is completed.

Gallery Guide

The vast gallery is organized in chronological order for the most part and the rooms, labelled with roman numerals, are equipped with explanatory cards in English. The Quadreria corridor is filled with masterpieces.

8 Coronation of the Virgin

This resplendent polyptych (1350) by Venice's leading 14th-century artist, Paolo Veneziano, is the first work in Room 1. Flanking the stunning Byzantine-inspired central piece are events depicted from the life of Christ.

9 Portrait of a Gentleman

Lorenzo Lotto's sombre image of a melancholic man of means in his study (1528) **(above)** may be a self-portrait (Room 7). Lotto was known for works of psychological insight.

10 Lion of St Mark with Saints John the Baptist, John the Evangelist, Mary Magdalene and Jerome

This marvellous canvas (in Room 23) by Cima di Conegliano depicts a winged lion flanked by four saints.

TOP 10 ⭐ Santa Maria Gloriosa dei Frari

A masterpiece of Venetian Gothic ecclesiastical architecture, this cavernous 15th-century church for Franciscan friars took more than 100 years to complete, along with its "brother" SS Giovanni e Paolo *(see p52)*, and a further 26 years for the consecration of the main altar. A wonderful series of art treasures is held within the deceptively gloomy interior, which is almost 100-m (330-ft) long and 50-m (165-ft) across, from priceless canvases by Titian and Bellini to tombs of doges and artists such as Canova.

1 Assumption of the Virgin

Titian's glowing 1518 depiction of the triumphant ascent of Mary **(left)** shows her robed in crimson accompanied by a semicircle of saints, while the 12 apostles are left gesticulating in wonderment below. This brilliant canvas on the high altar is the inevitable focus of the church.

Santa Maria Gloriosa dei Frari

2 Rood Screen

A beautifully carved blend of Renaissance and Gothic elements by Pietro Lombardo and Bartolomeo Bon (1475), the screen, also decorated with marble figures, divides the worship area and nave **(right)**.

5 Campanile

The robust 14th-century bell tower set into the church's left transept is the second tallest in Venice.

3 Choir Stalls

Unique for Venice, the original three tiers of 124 friars' seats deserve close examination for their fascinating inlaid woodwork. Crafted by Marco Cozzi in 1468, they clearly demonstrate the influence of northern European styles.

4 Madonna Enthroned with Saints

Tucked away in the sacristy, and still in its original engraved frame, is another delight for Bellini fans (1488). "It seems painted with molten gems," wrote Henry James of the triptych.

STATE ARCHIVES

The labyrinthine monastery and courtyards adjoining the church have been home to Venice's State Archives since the fall of the Republic. Its 300 rooms and approximately 70 km (43 miles) of shelves are loaded with precious records documenting the history of Venice right back to the 9th century, including the Golden Book register of the Venetian aristocracy. Scholars enter the building via the Oratorio di San Nicolò della Lattuga (1332), named after the miraculous recovery of a Procurator of San Marco thanks to the healing qualities of a lettuce (*lattuga*).

Canova's Mausoleum 6

This colossal monument **(right)**, based on Canova's Neo-Classical design for Titian's tomb, which was never built, was a tribute by the sculptor's followers in 1822.

7 Monument to Doge Francesco Foscari

This is a fine Renaissance tribute to the man responsible for Venice's mainland expansion. Foscari was the subject of Lord Byron's *The Two Foscari*, which was turned into an opera by Verdi.

Statue of John the Baptist 8

The inspirational wood statue from 1450 **(right)**, which was created especially for the church by artist Donatello (1386–1466), stands in the Florentine chapel. The emaciated carved figure is renowned for being particularly lifelike.

9 Monument to Titian

Titian was afforded special authorization for burial here after his death during the 1576 plague, although this sturdy mausoleum was not built for another 300 years.

Church Floorplan

10 Mausoleum of Doge Giovanni Pesaro

The monsters and black marble figures supporting the sarcophagus of this macabre Baroque monument prompted art critic John Ruskin to write "it seems impossible for false taste and base feeling to sink lower".

NEED TO KNOW

MAP L3 ▪ Campo dei Frari, San Polo ▪ 041 275 04 62 ▪ www.chorus venezia.org

Open 9am–6pm Mon–Sat, 1–6pm Sun; closed 1 Jan, Easter, 15 Aug, 25 Dec

Admission €3; Chorus Pass €12 (includes admission to 18 churches)

▪ There are some great cafés and eateries in Campo dei Frari.

▪ Youngsters will love the nativity scene with day–night lighting effects and moving figures at Christmas.

TOP 10 ⭐ The Rialto

The commercial hub of Venice, centred on the Rialto Bridge *(see p56)*, is as bustling today as it has always been – records tell of markets here since 1097. The area is also the city's historical heart and took its name from Rivoaltus, the high consolidated terrain that guaranteed early settlers flood-free premises. Most buildings, however, date from the 16th century, because a fire swept through Rialto in 1514. During Carnival the stall-holders don medieval costume to vie with each other for custom and only the new awnings and electronic cash registers hint at the modern world.

1 Fresh Produce Market

The market here is a treat for the senses, with artistic piles of luscious peaches and cherries, thorny artichokes and red chicory from Treviso. Fruit, vegetables and fish tend to be strictly seasonal **(above)**.

Rialto market alongside the Grand Canal

3 San Giacomo di Rialto

The oldest church in Venice claims to have a foundation set by a pious carpenter in the 5th century, although the present building is medieval. The Gothic portico and 24-hour clock are well worth a look.

4 Public Rostrum

New laws and names of criminals were announced atop this porphyry column **(right)**, supported by a stone figure known as *il gobbo* (hunchback).

2 Pescheria

Writhing eels, soft-shelled crabs, huge swordfish and crimson-fleshed fresh tuna are among the stars of the 1907 Neo-Gothic fish market hall **(above)**, barely out of reach of the scavenging seagulls.

5 Palazzo dei Camerlenghi

This lopsided 1525 palace once imprisoned debtors on the ground floor, while the top floors served as offices for the city *camerlenghi* (treasurers).

6 Gondola Ferry
A must for every visitor is a trip on the *traghetto* ferry across the Grand Canal **(left)** – one of only eight still in operation. Custom dictates that passengers should remain standing.

7 Banco Giro Arcade
Merchants from the East and the West gathered to exchange a variety of goods, including silks and spices, outside the city's first bank set up in 1157, which is now a wine bar.

PLACE NAMES

Rialto market's narrow alleyways carry names such as Orefici (goldsmiths), Pescaria (fishmongers) and Erberia (vegetables), because the same type of shops once stood together. Local eateries for market traders also had evocative names such as Scimia (Monkey) and Do Mori (Two Moors).

8 Ruga degli Orefici
This lovely covered passageway decorated with frescoes has been home to silversmiths, goldsmiths and silk traders since the 1300s.

9 Fabbriche Nuove
Uniformed *carabinieri* (police) patrol the elongated law courts along the Grand Canal. Designed in 1552–5 by Sansovino they are recognizable by their 25 plain arcades.

10 Grand Canal Views
The Erberia, right on the Grand Canal, makes a wonderful spot for boat-watching. Alternatively, wander on to the Rialto Bridge for a different vantage point **(below)**.

NEED TO KNOW

MAP P2 ■ San Polo ■ Fresh produce market: 7:30am–1pm Mon–Sat; Pescheria: 7:30am–1pm Tue–Sat

■ In addition to fresh fruit from the market, picnic supplies can be bought at the delicatessens and bakeries in the neighbourhood.

TOP 10 ⭐ Torcello

Some of the most breathtaking Byzantine mosaics in the world, found in the lagoon's oldest building, the Torcello basilica, reward those who visit this laid-back island, a beautiful 60-minute ferry ride from northern Venice. From the 5th century, mainlanders fleeing invading Lombards and Huns ventured across tidal flats to found a settlement that grew to 20,000 and lasted 1,000 years. However, few clues to the past remain, as the canals silted up, malaria decimated the population and the power base shifted to Venice once and for all. Today, Torcello is home to a handful of gardeners and fishermen.

Basilica Exterior ①

A miraculous survivor, this striking cathedral was founded in 639, but underwent radical restructuring in 1008. It retains its Romanesque form, light-brick walls and an arcaded 9th-century portico **(right)**.

② Doomsday Mosaics, Basilica

In these 12th–13th-century marvels **(above)**, the Last Judgment is dramatically depicted in superbly restored scenes of devils, angels, wild beasts and fires.

③ Apse Mosaics, Basilica

This moving 13th-century mosaic shows the Virgin in a blue robe with gold fringing, cradling her radiant child. Below are the 12 apostles standing in a meadow of flowers.

④ Iconostasis, Basilica

Marble panels show peacocks drinking at the fountain of eternal life

(left), small lions posing under a tree full of birds, while six columns support 15th-century paintings of the apostles with the Virgin.

⑤ Paving, Basilica

In vivid swirls of colours, rivalling the flooring in Basilica San Marco, are brilliant 11th-century tesserae of stone and glass. Cubes, semicircles and triangles are laid into square designs. The floor level was raised 30 cm (12 inches) during the basilica's reconstruction.

7 Campanile

The views from this simple 55-m (180-ft) bell tower **(left)** reach over the vast expanse of the lagoon, with its meandering canals and tidal flats, to the Adriatic Sea, Venice itself and even north to the Alps on a clear winter's day.

8 Throne of Attila

By popular belief this marble armchair **(below)** was the throne of the king of the Huns, though historical sources claim it was for the island's magistrates.

ATTILA THE HUN

The "Scourge of God", or the King of the Huns, ruled from AD 434 to 453 over an empire that stretched from the Alps and the Baltic towards the Caspian Sea. As part of his campaign against the Roman Empire, Attila attacked Milan, Verona and Padua, and refugees fled to Torcello. Burning the cathedral town of Aquileia gave him great satisfaction – his men raised a hill in Udine so he could enjoy the sight.

9 Museo dell'Estuario

An intriguing, if modest, collection of archaeological finds from the island and priceless treasures from the church are housed in the adjoining Gothic buildings.

NEED TO KNOW

MAP H1 ■ Boat line 12 from the Fondamente Nuove to Burano, then change to boat line 9

Basilica di Santa Maria dell'Assunta: 041 730 119; Open Mar–Oct: 10:30am–5:30pm daily; Nov–Feb: 10am–4:30pm daily; closed 1 Jan, 25 Dec. Admission €5

Campanile: Open Mar–Oct: 10:30am–5:30pm daily; Nov–Feb: 10am–5pm. Admission €5. Audio guide

Santa Fosca: Closed to visitors during services

Museo dell'Estuario: 041 730 761; Open Mar–Oct: 10:30am– 5:30pm Tue–Sun; Nov–Feb: 10am–5pm Tue–Sun; closed public hols. Admission €3

---

6 Santa Fosca

Alongside the basilica is this elegant church based on a Greek cross design, encircled by a five-sided colonnaded portico. The inside of the church is closed to visitors during services.

10 Locanda Cipriani

A favourite of American writer Ernest Hemingway, who stayed here in 1948, this guesthouse **(left)** has a quiet charm that has attracted VIPs since it opened in 1938 *(see p148)*.

★ Campo Santa Margherita

This cheery, picturesque square in the district of Dorsoduro is a hive of activity day in, day out. It owes its name to the Christian martyr St Margaret of Antioch, possibly a fictitious figure, but highly popular in medieval times. Patron saint of expectant mothers, she is depicted in a niche on the square's northern wall with her emblem, the dragon. The square's capacious form, exploited by local children on bicycles and in-line skates, is due to an ambitious enlargement project in the 1800s which opened up the south end by filling in canals.

1 Ex Chiesa di Santa Margherita

A writhing 14th-century dragon symbolizing the martyrdom of the saint enlivens the foot of the bell tower of the former church. It has been restored by the university as the Auditorium Santa Margherita.

2 Palazzo Foscolo-Corner

This beautiful palace is virtually unchanged since the 1300s and instantly distinguishable by its deep overhanging eaves. A striking Byzantine-style lunette, bearing an inset with the family crest, tops the entrance portal.

3 Scuola Grande dei Carmini

Glorious rooms (below), decorated with Tiepolo's masterpieces, are highlights of this confraternity. The upstairs ceiling shows *St Simon Stock Receiving the Scapular from the Virgin*.

Campo Santa Margherita

4 Calle del Forno

An unusual series of medieval-style projections from a first-floor dwelling, partly held up by brick columns, is one of the most interesting features of this busy thoroughfare leading to Piazzale Roma and the bus terminal. The street is named after a long-gone *forno* (bakery).

5 Scuola dei Varoteri

A splendid bas-relief of the Virgin sheltering a group of trades-men in adoration adorns the former tanners' guild dating from 1725. Because of its isolated position, it was once mistakenly thought to be the house of the city's executioner.

6 Chiesa di Santa Maria dei Carmini

This richly adorned church **(left)** survived Napoleon's suppression of the Carmelite order of monks in the adjoining monastery. Many of its 13th-century features are intact, such as the sculpted entrance porch.

RIO TERRÀ

Rio is a common name for canal, while *terrà* means filled-in. Dating back to the 1300s, the practice of filling in waterways was widespread in the 1800s to provide extra pedestrian space. Some were covered with low-slung arches to keep water flowing, exemplified by Via Garibaldi in Castello (see p111). Later campaigns encouraged the reverse procedure.

9 Corte del Fondaco

A charming covered passageway leads through to this minor courtyard where curious, low, bricked-in arches indicate the former site of a 1700s flour store. The name *fondaco* – or store – is derived from the Arabic word *fonduq*.

10 Rio Nuovo

Excavated in 1932–3 to form a shortcut from Piazzale Roma to the Grand Canal, the canal has been closed to *vaporetti* since the 1990s, due to building damage.

7 The "House of the Moor"

Shakespeare's *Othello* was based on Cristoforo Moro, who was sent to govern Cyprus from 1508. This house at No. 2615 is his former home.

8 Altana Terraces

These timber roof platforms **(right)** were common in Venetian palaces, used by women for bleaching their hair in the sun. They are now used for laundry and partying on summer evenings, and can be seen around Campo Santa Margherita.

NEED TO KNOW

MAP K5

Scuola Grande dei Carmini, Dorsoduro: 041 528 94 20 ▪ www. scuolagrandecarmini.it

Open 11am–5pm daily (Nov–Mar: 11am–4pm)

Admission €5

▪ Numerous pizza-slice outlets and bars serving *tramezzini* (sandwiches) and *panini* (rolls) make for a cheap lunch option.

TOP10 ⭐ Peggy Guggenheim Collection

The delightfully spacious, light-filled Collezione Peggy Guggenheim is home to works by more than 200 contemporary artists representing powerful avant-garde movements such as Cubism, Futurism and Surrealism. The landmark collection, put together by its far-sighted namesake, is housed in the 18th-century Palazzo Venier dei Leoni, known as the "unfinished palace" because of its one-storey construction. As well as the wonderful works of art on display inside the gallery, there is also a striking sculpture garden and the former home of Peggy Guggenheim to visit.

1 The Poet
A wonderful starting point is this portrait (1911) by legendary Spanish artist Pablo Picasso (1881–1973), from his early Cubist period. The figure is executed from a limited palette of ochre and dark browns.

2 Bird in Space
This polished brass sculpture (1932–40) was once classified by US customs as a "stair-rail" and was therefore subject to duty. Its creator was Romanian artist Constantin Brancusi (1876–1957).

3 Attirement of the Bride
This portrayal (1940) of an orange-robed bride assisted by mutant animals and humans **(below)** is by Max Ernst (1891–1976). The German Surrealist was married to Guggenheim from 1942 to 1946.

Peggy Guggenheim Collection

Key to Floorplan
- Gallery
- Nasher Sculpture Garden

4 Empire of Light

Magical light effects see darkened trees and a house silhouetted by a street lamp against a contrasting daytime sky with fluffy clouds in this work (1953–4) by René Magritte (1898–1967). The Belgian Surrealist was renowned for his eccentric subjects.

6 Woman Walking

This serene elongated form of a truncated female figure (1932), apparently inspired by Etruscan design, is the recognized trademark of the Swiss artist Alberto Giacometti (1901–66), a short-term participant in the Surrealist movement **(right)**.

7 The Moon Woman

This vibrant canvas (1942) starring a skeletal stick figure with an odd, padded curve is an early work by Jackson Pollock (1912–56), pre-dating his famous "drip" technique.

PEGGY GUGGENHEIM

This heir to a mining fortune (1898–1979) first came to Europe in 1921, quickly fitting into Bohemian Paris. Resolving to "buy a picture a day", she amassed a contemporary art collection before she made Venice her home in 1947. She is fondly remembered by locals here for her faithful dogs and for owning the city's last private gondola.

8 Mobile

This simple masterpiece of movement (1941) by Alexander Calder (1898–1976), which gave its name to all mobiles, hangs in the atrium of Guggenheim's house.

9 Angel of the City

Set on steps leading to the terrace, this bronze horse and rider (1948) by Italian sculptor Marino Marini (1901–80) greet passing boats.

NEED TO KNOW

MAP D5 ■ Fondamenta Venier dei Leoni, Dorsoduro 704 (2nd entrance Calle S Cristoforo, Dorsoduro 701) ■ 041 240 54 11 ■ www.guggenheim-venice.it ■ Coffee shop ■ Audio guides ■ No flash photography ■ Shop

Open 10am–6pm Wed–Mon; Closed 25 Dec

Admission €15

■ Take a break on the café's shady verandah for a light snack or a meal.

■ Enjoy the view from the terrace, which looks onto the Grand Canal.

5 Magic Garden

This deliberately child-like piece (1926) by Paul Klee (1879–1940) features blurry shapes and sketched-in faces and buildings.

10 Three Standing Figures

Beautifully placed in the Nasher Sculpture Garden, these sculptures (1953) by Henry Moore (1898–1986) were inspired by Italian bell towers.

The Top 10
of Everything

The world-famous Rialto Bridge, one of
four bridges spanning the Grand Canal

🔟 Outstanding Venetians

1 Marco Polo

Legendary Cathay and the kingdom of the mighty Kublai Khan took pride of place in the great explorer Marco Polo's best-selling account of his 20-year odyssey to the Far East, *Book of the Marvels of the World*. Son of a Venetian merchant, Polo (1254–1324) is responsible for the introduction of pasta and window blinds to the western world.

Marco Polo

2 Antonio Vivaldi

Vivaldi (1678–1741) was both an accomplished musician and an influential Baroque composer. Of his 500 concertos, *The Four Seasons* is the best known. J S Bach was a noted fan and transcribed ten of the Italian's concertos. Vivaldi spent extended periods teaching music at the Pietà home for girls *(see p109)*.

3 Giacomo Casanova

This marvellous romantic figure (1725–98) was variously a diplomat, scholar, trainee priest, adventurer, gambler, notary's clerk, violinist, womanizer, exile, millionaire, writer and spy. Casanova was imprisoned in the Doge's Palace *(see pp16–19)* on charges of being a magician, from where he effected an infamously daring escape.

Giacomo Casanova

4 Claudio Monteverdi

This late Renaissance madrigalist (1567–1643) is attributed with the introduction of the solo voice to theatre. His opera *Proserpina Rapita* was the first to be performed in Venice. After long periods at the court of the Gonzagas, he accepted an appointment at the Basilica San Marco and worked for the Scuola Grande di San Rocco *(see p89)*.

5 John Cabot

Italian navigator Giovanni Caboto, or John Cabot (1450–99), and his sons were authorized by Henry VII of England to search for new lands with the aim of furthering trade. Believing himself on the northeast coast of Asia, he discovered Newfoundland in Canada and claimed it for England, opening up cod fishing.

6 Elena Lucrezia Corner Piscopia

It was inconceivable for the church in 1678 that a woman should teach religion, so the University of Padua awarded this child prodigy and the first woman graduate (1646–84) a degree in philosophy, instead of one in theology to which she aspired.

7 Daniele Manin

Organizer of the 1848 rebellion against Austrian rule, the Venetian patriot (1804–57) is commemorated by a statue in Campo Manin. An independent "republic" was declared and survived 17 months of bombardments and even cholera, concluding with Manin's exile to Paris.

8 Paolo Sarpi

When the pope excommunicated Venice for insubordination, involving restrictions on church construction and the refusal to hand over two priests on criminal charges, Sarpi (1552–1623) resolved the rupture. A patriot and theologian, he was an advocate of division between State and Church.

Caterina Cornaro

⑨ Caterina Cornaro

This Venetian noblewoman (1454–1510) married the king of Cyprus then allegedly poisoned him, thus securing the strategic island for Venice. Her return to the city was an occasion of great pomp, recalled to this day in a waterborne procession during the Regata Storica (see p72). Cornaro's reward was the hilltown of Asolo.

⑩ Luigi Nono

This musician (1924–90) made milestone progress in the field of electronic music, and an archive named after him was set up in Venice in 1993. A committed Communist, his works were often provocative.

Avant-garde composer Luigi Nono

TOP 10 FOREIGN COMMUNITIES

Frenchman Claude Monet's painting of the Grand Canal

1 Greeks
Here since 1498, the Greeks are the longest surviving group, still active with their own church.

2 Armenians
Fleeing Turkish invasion, in 1717 the close-knit religious group was granted an island by the Republic (see p124).

3 Dalmatians (Slavs)
Traders from a historical region of Croatia, whose boats gave their name to the Riva degli Schiavoni (see p109).

4 Turks
Although the Turks were enemies of Venice, the Republic still rented them a trade centre between 1621 and 1898.

5 Jews
The Spanish Inquisition triggered the move here for many Jews expelled from other European countries.

6 Albanians
Calle degli Albanesi near Piazza San Marco is named in honour of this large 15th-century community.

7 Germans
The former German trade head-quarters Fondaco dei Tedeschi attracted artists such as Albrecht Dürer.

8 British
Extended sojourns here were de rigueur for the British upper class during the 19th-century Grand Tour.

9 French
Impressionist painter Claude Monet and writers Théophile Gautier and Marcel Proust were attracted to the city in the late 1800s.

10 Americans
Leading literary figures and patrons of the arts have paid long-term visits since the 19th century.

🔟 Writers and Venice

Teatro Comunale Carlo Goldoni

1 Carlo Goldoni
"Italy's Molière" (1707–93) is celebrated at the Venetian theatre named in his honour (see p62). Performances of his lively, witty comedies are staged in Venetian dialect and peopled with recognizable local characters. The prolific playwright moved to Paris and was rewarded with a royal pension, but he died destitute due to the French Revolution.

2 Thomas Mann
The sombre 1912 novel *Death in Venice* was both written and set in Venice and the Lido resort by the German Nobel Prize-winner (1875–1955). It tells the story of an ageing writer in dire need of relaxation who visits the city, but in the wake of an impossible infatuation slowly succumbs to the spreading cholera epidemic and dies.

3 William Shakespeare
Although he never visited Italy, let alone Venice, the English Bard (1564–1616) used accounts by contemporary travellers for the plots of *The Merchant of Venice* and *Othello*, portraying a city buzzing with trade and intrigue. *Romeo and Juliet* is set in nearby Verona (see p130).

William Shakespeare

4 Thomas Coryate
The very first English-language traveller to write a detailed description of Venice, this eccentric gentleman from Somerset, England (1577–1617) compiled *Crudities, with Observations of Venice* (1611): "Such is the rarenesse of the situation of Venice, that it doth even amaze and drive into admiration all strangers that upon their first arrival behold the same."

5 Johann Wolfgang von Goethe
The story goes that this German literary giant (1749–1832) had his first ever view of the sea from Venice's Campanile. His first visit to the city and Italy was an experience of personal renewal. The account, published as *Italian Journey* (1786–8), is considered an early classic of travel literature.

Johann Wolfgang von Goethe

6 Lord Byron
Eccentricities such as a menagerie of foxes and monkeys, not to mention swimming feats in the Grand Canal, made the English Romantic poet (1788–1824) something of a legend during his three-year sojourn here. His Venice-inspired work included *The Two Foscari* and the fourth canto of his autobiographical work *Childe Harold's Pilgrimage*.

7 John Ruskin
The meticulous, if opinionated, labour of love of this British art critic (1819–1900), *The Stones of Venice*, was the first work to focus the attention of visitors on the city's unique architectural heritage

and Gothic style, as opposed to the art. The book was largely the outcome of an 1849 visit to the city.

⑧ Henry James

The leitmotif of this US novelist (1843–1916) was the contrast between what he saw as the spontaneity of the New World and the staidness of Europe. Between 1872 and 1909 he compiled *Italian Hours*, a "travel diary", with plenty of comments on Venice.

Ernest Hemingway

⑨ Ernest Hemingway

This US Nobel Prize-winner (1899–1961) experienced Italy as a volunteer ambulance driver in World War I (recounted in *A Farewell to Arms*) and was wounded near Treviso. *Across the River and into the Trees* is set in Harry's Bar (see p25).

⑩ Charles Dickens

The great English novelist (1812–70) spent a brief period in Venice during a tour of Italy, and the city inspired a dream sequence in his work *Pictures from Italy* (1846).

Illustration from "An Italian Dream" in Dickens's *Pictures from Italy*

TOP 10 BACKGROUND READS

***Death in Venice* film adaptation**

1 Venice, Jan Morris
An expert account of the delights of the city and its maritime history.

2 Venice, an Anthology Guide, Milton Grundy
A guide around town, seen through the eyes of famous writers.

3 Ruskin's Venice, editor Arnold Whittick
A very readable version of Ruskin's landmark work.

4 Death in Venice, Thomas Mann
A portrayal of desire and decadence amid the fog.

5 Stone Virgin, Barry Unsworth
A mystery involving the 15th-century statue of a famous courtesan.

6 Casanova, or the Art of Happiness, Lydia Flem
An inspired biography of the famous seducer (see p44).

7 Dead Lagoon, Michael Dibdin
Detective Aurelio Zen navigates Venice's murky waters fraught with unease and intrigue.

8 The Architecture of Venice, Deborah Howard
An unbeatable architectural classic.

9 Venice: A Maritime Republic, Frederic C. Lane
A comprehensive history of the city's maritime prowess.

10 Acqua Alta, Donna Leon
From the best-selling mystery series featuring detective Guido Brunetti.

Artists in Venice

The Madonna of the Meadow (1505)
by Giovanni Bellini

1 Giovanni Bellini

With his father Jacopo and brother Gentile, Giovanni Bellini (1430–1516) made Venice one of the world's greatest centres of Renaissance art. His anatomy studies added great precision to his work. His trademarks are radiant Madonnas, serene St Peters and brilliant satiny robes.

2 Titian (Tiziano Vecellio)

A native of the Cadore region, whose awe-inspiring Dolomite peaks often feature in his highly coloured dynamic compositions, Titian (1488–1576) came to Venice when young and studied under Giovanni Bellini.

3 Canaletto (Giovanni Antonio Canal)

Famous for his landscapes of Venice and England, Canaletto (1697–1768) thrived under the patronage of the British consul Joseph Smith. Unfortunately, very few of his paintings can be seen in Venice.

4 Jacopo Tintoretto

The great Mannerist of the late Renaissance, Tintoretto (1518–94) produced huge, glowing canvases, seen at his main showcase the Scuola Grande di San Rocco (see p89), as well as his parish church Madonna dell'Orto (see p53).

5 Paolo Veronese

Foremost painter of the Venetian School, Veronese (1528–88) created huge canvases in classical settings and teeming with people. They are on display in the Doge's Palace (see pp16–19) and the Chiesa di San Sebastiano (see p98).

6 Giambattista Tiepolo

Tiepolo (1696–1770) is admired for his luminous poetic frescoes from the Rococo period, such as

View of the Grand Canal (late 1720s) by Canaletto

hose he was commissioned to paint on the ceiling of the Scuola Grande dei Carmini in Dorsoduro *(see p38)*. The villas near Vicenza also feature his work; however, his best work is in the Residenz, Würzburg.

7 Vittorio Carpaccio

This Renaissance master (1465–1525) delighted in remarkably detailed scenes of daily life in contemporary Venice. His original narrative style and marvellous command of light characterize his many cycles on display at the Accademia galleries *(see p31)* and the Scuola di San Giorgio degli Schiavoni *(see pp55)*.

8 Giorgione

A native of Castelfranco Veneto, Giorgione (1477–1510) came to Venice when young to serve as an apprentice under Giovanni Bellini. In his brief life, he produced memorable mood works that he never signed. One of his most famous works, *The Tempest*, can be seen in the Accademia *(see p30)*.

Virgin and Child (1504) by Giorgione

9 Pietro Longhi

Longhi (1702–85) painted witty scenes of the everyday life of the well-to-do folk in Venice. Examples of his work can be admired at the Fondazione Querini Stampalia *(see p54)*, as well as in Ca' Rezzonico *(see p50)*. Many figures are wearing the traditional Venetian mask.

10 Francesco Guardi

A prolific landscape painter, Guardi (1712–93) successfully captured the light and atmosphere of Venice in decline. People are depicted as insignificant and powerless against landscapes that incorporate the lagoon and islands. His canvases are on display at Ca' Rezzonico *(see p50)*.

TOP 10 VENICE ARCHITECTS

Chiesa del Santissimo Redentore, by Andrea Palladio

1 Jacopo Sansovino *(1486–1570)*
Outstanding architect who trained under – and took his name from – sculptor Andrea Sansovino. Examples of Jacopo's work are the Libreria *(see p22)* and Zecca.

2 Andrea Palladio *(1508–80)*
Regarded as one of the most influential architects of the western world, Palladio designed Classical villas in the Veneto and churches in Venice.

3 Baldassare Longhena *(1598–1682)*
Longhena's masterpiece, Santa Maria della Salute, was designed when he was just 26, but his flamboyant style is also seen in Ca' Rezzonico *(see p50)*.

4 Pietro Lombardo *(1435–1515)*
Lombardy native Pietro was director of works at the Doge's Palace. His trademark leafy bas-relief pattern is also seen at Santa Maria dei Miracoli *(see p104)*.

5 Mauro Coducci *(c.1440–1504)*
The Renaissance designs of Lombardy native Coducci can be seen in Palazzo Vendramin-Calergi *(see p69)*.

6 Bartolomeo Bon *(1374–1464)*
Sculptor/architect Bon's designs were the basis for the church and Scuola di San Rocco and the Ca' d'Oro *(see p50)*.

7 Michele Sanmicheli *(1484–1559)*
Original military fortification designs by this Mannerist architect are found in his home town of Verona.

8 Antonio Da Ponte *(1512–95)*
This engineer and architect is well known for the Rialto Bridge *(see p56)*.

9 Giannantonio Selva *(1757–1819)*
In Venice, Selva is best known for the elegant Fenice theatre *(see p62)*.

10 Carlo Scarpa *(1906–78)*
Modernist Scarpa reorganized both the Accademia and the Querini Stampalia along Japanese-inspired lines.

🔟 Venice Palaces

Ca' Rezzonico

1 Doge's Palace
See pp16–19.

2 Ca' d'Oro
The original lapis lazuli, vermilion and gold façade has long faded, but the breathtaking Gothic delicacy of this "golden palace" is intact, with exquisite marble tracery and arcaded loggias crafted by 15th-century stonemasons *(see p103)*.

Ca' d'Oro

3 Ca' Foscari
MAP L5 ▪ Calle Foscari, Dorsoduro 3246 ▪ Open for pre-booked guided tours only ▪ www.unive.it

Set on a strategic bend of the Grand Canal, this excellent example of late Gothic architecture has a series of mullioned windows facing the water, surmounted by an Istrian stone frieze. Once home to the long-ruling Doge Francesco Foscari, today it is part of the University of Venice.

4 Ca' Rezzonico
MAP L5 ▪ Fondamenta Rezzonico, Dorsoduro 3136 ▪ Open 10am–5pm Wed–Mon (to 6pm Apr–Oct) ▪ Admission charge ▪ www.visitmuve.it

This glittering palace adorned with Tiepolo ceiling frescoes, majestic Murano glass chandeliers and elaborate carved period furniture is now home to the Museum of 18th-century Venetian Life.

5 Palazzo Vendramin-Calergi
This stately Renaissance residence by architects Lombardo and Coducci was home to a string of noble families including the Cretan merchant Calergi in 1589. Another famed tenant was composer Richard Wagner, who spent his final years here. The palace is now home to the glittering City Casino *(see p69)*.

6 Ca' Dario
Framed multicoloured round stones *(tondi)* embellish this privately owned, asymmetrical palace dating from 1486. It was built for Giovanni Dario, ambassador to Constantinople, where he negotiated a peace treaty bringing long-term hostilities between Venice and the Turks to a temporary halt *(see p25)*.

⑦ Palazzo Mastelli

MAP D1 ■ Rio della Madonna dell'Orto, Cannaregio 3932 ■ Closed to public

This eclectic delight, on a peaceful back canal of Cannaregio, was the abode of three merchant brothers from Morea on the Peloponnese from 1112. Their turbaned likenesses in stone adorn neighbouring Campo dei Mori *(see p104)*. Lions, birds and a prominent camel can be picked out on the Gothic façade.

⑧ Palazzi Contarini degli Scrigni e Corfu

MAP B5 ■ Calle Contarini Corfu, Dorsoduro 1057 ■ Closed to public

A 15th-century residence, enlarged by architect Vincenzo Scamozzi for the 17th-century proprietor Contarini "of the coffers" *(scrigni)*, so-called for the vast wealth of his family. The roof-top "folly" acted as a useful observatory for astronomers.

⑨ Palazzo Barbaro

MAP M6 ■ Rio dell'Orso, S Marco 2840 ■ Closed to public

Cole Porter, Diaghilev, Monet and Whistler are just a few former guests of this private double palace, courtesy of the 19th-century Curtis family from Boston. Henry James wrote *The Aspern Papers* here and used it as the setting for *The Wings of a Dove (see p47)*.

⑩ Palazzo Pisani-Moretta

MAP M4 ■ Ramo Pisani e Barbarigo, S Polo 2766 ■ Open for private functions only

Venue of a fabulous masked ball during Carnival, when VIP guests glide up in gondolas to the candlelit Gothic façade on the Grand Canal. Tiepolo and Guarana contributed to the interior Baroque decorations.

Palazzo Pisani-Moretta

TOP 10 ARCHITECTURAL FEATURES OF A PALAZZO

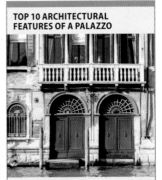

Typical canal entrance

1 Piano Nobile
The high-ceilinged first floor of a palazzo hosts the sumptuous salons and family's living quarters.

2 Façade
Usually fronting a canal, this was the only exterior wall decorated with a costly stone overlay to impress visitors.

3 Funnel-Shaped Chimneys
These and many other variations punctuate rooftops, their long shafts often running along outside walls.

4 Kitchen
This was always located on the ground floor for practical reasons.

5 Canal Entrance
Where the family's private gondolas were moored and visitors were received.

6 Central Well
This received filtered rain water for the palazzo's main water supply.

7 Entrance Portal
The importance of the main entrance was usually indicated by the distinctive family crest.

8 Enclosed Courtyard
This bustling area, usually with store rooms, was often used for the family's business transactions.

9 Altana Roof Terrace-Platform
These open-air areas were traditionally used for hanging out the washing or bleaching hair in the sun.

10 Land Access
Private gondolas rendered this relatively unimportant and hence, a narrow alley sufficed in its stead.

🔟 Venice Churches

① Basilica San Marco
See pp12–15.

② Santa Maria Gloriosa dei Frari
See pp32–3.

Santi Giovanni e Paolo

③ Santi Giovanni e Paolo
MAP E3 ■ Campo SS Giovanni e Paolo, Castello ■ Open 9am–6pm Mon–Sat, noon–6pm Sun ■ Admission charge ■ www.basilicasantigiovanniepaolo.it

The monumental tombs of 25 doges take pride of place in this Gothic giant, built by Dominican friars from the 13th to 15th centuries. Among them is the tribute to Pietro Mocenigo for his valorous struggle to defend Venice's eastern colonies against the Turks (west wall). Inside are splendid paintings by Veronese and a polyptych (1465) by Giovanni Bellini.

④ Santa Maria dei Miracoli
A favourite among Venetians for weddings, Pietro Lombardo's showcase (1481–9) is resplendent again after restoration to deal with rising damp. The problem is not new – in Renaissance times marble slabs were affixed to the brick exterior with a cavity left for air flow. The ceiling gleams with gilt miniatures of holy figures *(see p104)*.

⑤ San Zaccaria
MAP F4 ■ Campo S Zaccaria, Castello ■ Open 10am–noon, 4–6pm Mon–Sat, 4–6pm Sun & public hols ■ Admission charge (chapels & crypt)

An intricately decorated 15th-century façade by Coducci and, inside, Giovanni Bellini's superb *Madonna and Saints* (1505) are highlights of this 9th-century church. The adjoining convent, now a police station, used to host puppet shows to entertain the nuns.

⑥ San Giorgio Maggiore
MAP F5 ■ Isola di S Giorgio Maggiore ■ Open daily (times can vary) ■ Admission charge (bell tower)

Palladio's harmoniously proportioned church (1566–1610), inspired by Greek temple design, stands across the water from Piazza San Marco. The interior is offset by two dynamic paintings by Tintoretto from 1594, *The Last Supper* and *Gathering the Manna*, on the chancel walls. The bell tower offers views over Venice. Don't miss the monks' Gregorian chants every Sunday at 11am.

⑦ Santa Maria della Salute
MAP D5 ■ Campo della Salute, Dorsoduro ■ Open 9am–noon, 3–5pm daily ■ Admission charge (sacristy)

A remarkable Baroque church dominating the southernmost entrance to the Grand Canal, its silhouette has become one of Venice's most well-known landmarks. Designed by Longhena in 1630, it has a spacious, light-filled interior, while the altar houses a precious Byzantine icon. Dramatic works by Titian and Tintoretto can be appreciated in the sacristy.

8 Chiesa di San Sebastiano

Renaissance painter Paolo Veronese (1528–88) spent a large proportion of his life joyously decorating the ceiling, walls, organ doors and altar of this unassuming 16th-century church, and was buried among his colourful masterpieces *(see p98)*.

9 Madonna dell'Orto

MAP D1 ■ Campo Madonna dell'Orto, Cannaregio ■ Open 10am–5pm Mon–Sat, noon–5pm Sun ■ Admission charge ■ www.madonnadellorto.org

Huge canvases by devout parishioner Tintoretto enhance this graceful Gothic church. Two 1546 master-pieces flank the high altar, the gruesome *Last Judgment* and the soaring grandeur of *The Making of the Golden Calf*.

Madonna dell'Orto

10 San Pantalon

MAP K4 ■ Campo S Pantalon, Dorsoduro ■ Open 10am–noon, 1–3pm Mon–Sat ■ www.sanpantalon.it

Two treasures lurk behind a ramshackle façade: a nail from the True Cross in a rich Gothic altar and the overwhelming ceiling (1680–1704) by Gian Antonio Fumiani, a labour of love that ended when he purportedly plunged from the scaffolding to his death.

TOP 10 SHRINES AND TABERNACLES

Flowers at a shrine to St Anthony

1 Sottoportego de la Madonna
MAP D3 ■ Sant' Aponal, S Polo
Pope Alexander III took refuge here from Emperor Barbarossa in 1177.

2 Gondolier's Shrine
MAP R5 ■ Ponte della Paglia, S Marco
A 1583 Madonna greets boats approaching the bridge.

3 Corte Nova
MAP G4 ■ Castello
Painted images over a lace-trimmed mantlepiece.

4 Covered Passageway
MAP F4 ■ Calle Zorzi, Castello
The Virgin's protection has been implored here against plague and enemy attacks.

5 Scuola Grande della Misericordia
MAP D2 ■ Cannaregio
Carvings of laden boats seek protection for the ferries, which set out from here.

6 Corte de Ca' Sarasina
MAP H5 ■ Castello
Shrine dating back to the 1600s in memory of the dead.

7 St Anthony
MAP D2 ■ Calle Larga, Cannaregio
This 1668 "wardrobe" is full of fresh flower offerings.

8 Ponte del Fontego
MAP F3 ■ Campo S Giustina, Castello
A Neo-Classical bridge featuring gondola bas-reliefs.

9 Gondola Traghetto Point
MAP L4 ■ S Tomà, S Polo
Madonna on a pole in the Grand Canal.

10 Boatmen's Pole
Tabernacle midway on the San Giuliano–Venice channel.

⑩ **Museums and Galleries**

① Accademia Galleries
See pp30–31.

② Museo del Merletto
MAP H1 ▪ **Piazza Baldassare Galuppi 187, Burano** ▪ **Open Apr–Oct: 10am–6pm Tue–Sun (to 5pm Nov–Mar)** ▪ **Admission charge**

A must for craft-lovers is the lacemaking island of Burano and this precious display of more than 200 rare lace items, documenting a 500-year history.

③ Museo del Vetro
MAP G2 ▪ **Fondamenta Giustiniani 8, Murano** ▪ **Open Apr–Oct: 10am–6pm daily (to 5pm Nov–Mar)** ▪ **Admission charge** ▪ **www.visitmuve.it**

A phenomenal chandelier from 1864, constructed from 356 handmade pieces, weighing 330 kg (730 lb) and measuring nearly 7 m (23 ft) in circumference and 4-m (13-ft) high, is the star of this glass museum in the Palazzo Giustiniani. Other exhibits include Phoenician phials, blown vases, ruby chalices, exquisite mirrors and

Murano glassware at Museo del Vetro

the famed kaleidoscopic beads that were once traded worldwide.

④ Palazzo Grassi
This landmark collection of contemporary art (see p82), housed in a palace on the Grand Canal, is renewed on a regular basis. The inspirational sister gallery is Punta della Dogana (see p98).

⑤ Fondazione Querini Stampalia
MAP R4 ▪ **Campo S Maria Formosa, Castello 5252** ▪ **Open 10am–6pm Tue–Sun** ▪ **Admission charge** ▪ **www.querinistampalia.org**

This unmissable Renaissance palace was the bequest of Giovanni Querini in 1868, the last member of the illustrious dynasty, on the condition that the library be made available "particularly in the evenings for the convenience of scholars". The immaculately restored palace-museum houses fascinating scenes of public and private life by Gabriel Bella and Pietro Longhi, as well as Carlo Scarpa's Modernist creations.

6 Museo Correr

A tremendous number of priceless artworks and a miscellany of items on Venice's history are housed in this fine museum on Piazza San Marco *(see p22)*.

Museo Correr

7 Ca' Pesaro Galleria d'Arte Moderna

MAP N1 ■ Fondamenta Ca' Pesaro, S Croce 2076 ■ Open Apr–Oct 10am–6pm Tue–Sun (to 5pm Nov–Mar) ■ Admission charge ■ www.visitmuve.it

A Baroque triumph of a palace whose interior, in contrast, houses works by European 19th- and 20th-century masters such as Marc Chagall and Gustave Klimt.

November 1870 by Telemaco Signorini in the Ca' Pesaro Galleria

8 Scuola di San Giorgio degli Schiavoni

MAP F4 ■ Calle dei Furlani, Castello 3259 ■ Closed Mon am & Sun pm ■ Admission charge

The finest work of Vittorio Carpaccio can be seen at the confraternity of the Slavs (Schiavoni). Slaying the dragon is one of the scenes from the lives of Dalmatian saints, who were executed in 1502.

9 Scuola Grande di San Rocco

The San Rocco confraternity has now been turned into a gallery to display its spectacular collection of works by Tintoretto. The artist won the commission hands down – not content with a sketch, he completed an entire canvas. He then spent 23 years devoting himself to the cycle of 60 inspired Old and New Testament scenes, culminating in the breathtaking *Crucifixion* (1565). These masterpieces are the crowning glory of Tintoretto's life work *(see p89)*.

Doge's ceremonial barge at the Museo Storico Navale

10 Museo Storico Navale

MAP G4 ■ Campo S Biagio, Castello 2148 ■ Open 8:45am–1:30pm Mon–Fri (to 1pm Sat) ■ Admission charge ■ www.marina.difesa.it

Watercraft galore are found here, and almost an entire floor is dedicated to the golden age of the Venetian Republic's naval past. However, the highlight is the replica of the Doge's ceremonial barge, *Bucintoro*, decorated with allegorical statues.

🔟 Bridges

1 Bridge of Sighs
MAP R5

This evocatively named bridge (known as Ponte dei Sospiri by locals) once led convicts from the beautiful Doge's Palace to the horrors of the adjacent prisons *(see p17)*.

2 Rialto Bridge
MAP P3

The design of this most famous Venetian bridge at the narrowest point of the Grand Canal was hotly contested – leading 16th-century architects Michelangelo, Sansovino and Palladio entered the competition, but lost out to Antonio da Ponte.

There were two previous bridges on this site; a flimsy timber bridge that collapsed in 1444 under the weight of a crowd, then a drawbridge, which would be raised for the passage of tall-masted sailing ships *(see p34)*.

3 Ponte dei Tre Archi
MAP B1

A favourite subject for artists, this unusual three-arched high bridge dating from 1688 crosses the Cannaregio canal close to where it joins the lagoon. It was the work of engineer Andrea Tirali, nicknamed Tiranno (the tyrant) by his employees.

Ponte dei Tre Archi

4 Ponte degli Scalzi
MAP J1

One of the city's most marvellous lookout points, over fascinating palaces and boats, can be found at the highest point of this elegant 40-m- (130-ft-) long bridge, which rises 7 m (23 ft) above the Grand Canal. Named after the nearby monastery of bare-footed monks, this 1934 structure in Istrian stone by Eugenio Miozzi replaced an Austrian-built iron bridge.

Ponte della Libertà

(5) Ponte della Libertà
MAP A1

Truth and irony combine in the name of this 3.6-km (2-mile) "Bridge of Freedom": the first full link between the mainland and Venice was put in place in 1933, when Italy was living under Fascism. The construction was preceded 86 years earlier by the Austrian-built railway bridge across the lagoon. Before that, the city relied entirely on boats.

(6) Ponte dei Pugni
MAP K5

Pugni (fistfights) between rival clans took place here until 1705 when they were outlawed for their violence. Stone footprints marked the starting point of the combat, but contestants usually ended up in the canal.

(7) Bridge with No Parapet
MAP D2

One of only two remaining bridges with no side protection, this one spans a quiet side canal in Cannaregio. The other is the Ponte del Diavolo on Torcello.

(8) Ponte delle Tette
MAP M2

When an increase in the practice of sodomy was recorded in the 1400s, the city's prostitutes were encouraged to display their feminine wares at the windows over the "Bridge of Breasts".

(9) Tre Ponti
MAP B3

Not three but five interlocking bridges span the Rio Novo canal near Piazzale Roma. The timber and stone structures afford views taking in 13 other bridges.

Ponte degli Scalzi

(10) Ponte di Costituzione
MAP B3

Also known as the Ponte di Calatrava, after its designer Santiago Calatrava, this fourth Grand Canal is modelled on a gondola's hull. It has attracted criticism since its 2008 inauguration due its minimalist modern design and the high cost of construction.

Bridge with No Parapet, over Rio di San Felice

🔟 Off the Beaten Track

1 Cloister of Sant'Apollonia

MAP R4 ▪ **Ponte della Canonica, Castello 4312** ▪ **Open 10am–5pm Tue–Sun**

Literally steps away from Piazza San Marco, Venice's only original Romanesque cloister boasts a lovely courtyard with twin-columned arcades. A quiet spot, it is part of the Museo Diocesano d'Arte Sacra.

Sant'Elena

Cloister of Sant'Apollonia

2 Rio Terrà Rampani

MAP M2 ▪ **San Polo**

Just around the corner from Ponte delle Tette (Bridge of Breasts; see p57) is this quiet thoroughfare. Referred to as the "Carampane" (Ca' Rampani), it has been Venice's red-light district since 1421. The city had some 11,600 officially registered courtesans in the 1500s.

3 Sant'Elena

MAP H6

Located in the far eastern extremity of Venice, this quiet residential islet has marvellous shady parkland on the waterfront. Children can enjoy the skating rink and playground while parents relax at laidback cafés.

4 Celestia to Bacini Walkway

MAP G3 ▪ **Castello**

This unusual walkway clings to a perimeter wall of the ancient Arsenale shipyard in a rather neglected zone of Castello. It makes for an atmospheric walk, offering marvellous views over the lagoon and leading to a cluster of old workers' dwellings.

5 Corte dell'Anatomia

MAP L2 ▪ **S Croce**

This peaceful courtyard was named after the anatomy theatre that existed here in 1368. Much later, in 1671, in neighbouring Campo San Giacomo dell'Orio, a College of Anatomy was established in what is now a separate building with an attractive trellis draped with vines.

Calle del Paradiso

(Jesuit) church, it is flanked by the cavernous Crociferi complex, erstwhile monastery, then barracks, now student lodgings. Wander inside to admire the cloisters and the canal-side café.

8 Corte del Duca Sforza
MAP L6 ■ San Marco

This picturesque courtyard, which opens on to the Grand Canal, is surprisingly well hidden. It takes its name from the Duke of Milan who took over a partially constructed palace here in 1461, though work went no further than the diamond-point ashlar on the façade. The artist Titian used the building as a studio while he was working on the Doge's Palace *(see pp16–19)*.

9 Campo della Celestia
MAP G3 ■ Castello

Now a tranquil residential spot, back in the 1200s this square saw plenty of comings and goings due to the riotous behaviour of the sisters in the Cistercian convent. The first archive of city affairs was established here under Napoleon.

6 Calle del Paradiso
MAP R3 ■ Castello, San Lio

This attractive alley just off the busy San Lio thoroughfare is lined with medieval-style overhangs, as well as restaurants and shops. The name comes from the delightful lopsided, sculptured 15th-century arch depicting the Virgin and her devotees at the end.

7 Campo dei Gesuiti
MAP E2 ■ Cannaregio

A favourite spot for children to play in, this is a spacious neighbourhood square. In addition to the Gesuiti

10 Campo della Maddalena
MAP D2 ■ Cannaregio

Just off the main thoroughfare Strada Nova, you will find this lovely raised square. It is often used as a film location, due to the fact that it remains all but unchanged since medieval times. Its modest houses are topped with a fascinating range of chimneys.

Unspoilt and appealing Campo della Maddalena

🔟 Places for Children

The Giardini in Castello, a great place for children to let off steam

① Play Areas

Children tired of art and architecture can release their energy at well-equipped playgrounds with slides, swings and frames at Parco Savorgnan near Ponte delle Guglie in Cannaregio and the fenced-in waterfront park at Giardini in Castello *(see p111)*. The vast shady green expanse of Sant'Elena even boasts a modest skating rink and an artificial climbing wall. Otherwise, make friends with the city kids as they kick footballs or cycle around Campo San Polo *(see p89)* of an afternoon.

② Ferry Trips

Restful for adults, exciting for youngsters, the varied boat lines are an ideal way for families to appreciate the joys of the city. Get older children to plan trips on the route maps, but avoid the outside seating on the *vaporetto* with toddlers. For an extended trip, take the majestic double-decker *motonave* over to Lido and Punta Sabbioni *(see p119)*.

③ Glassmaking Demonstrations

Magic moments are guaranteed as children are transfixed by skilful craftsmen blowing blobs of molten glass into fine vases, or moulding coloured rods into myriad animal shapes. Small workshops are dotted all over Venice, while Murano has more large-scale furnaces – demonstrations are free, on the condition that you stroll through the showroom afterwards *(see p117)*.

④ Museo di Storia Naturale

MAP L1 ▪ Salizzada del Fondaco dei Turchi, S Croce 1730 ▪ 041 275 02 06 ▪ Open Jun–Oct: 10am–6pm Tue–Sun; Nov–May: 9am–5pm Tue–Fri, 10am–6pm Sat & Sun ▪ Admission ▪ www.visitmuve.it

The star of the marvellous natural history museum is a 3.6-m- (12-ft-) tall, 7-m- (23-ft-) long skeleton of the dinosaur Ouranosaurus nigeriensis, found in the Sahara Desert by the explorer Giancarlo Ligabue. Don't miss the aquarium.

Museo di Storia Naturale

Boat in the Museo Storico Navale

5 Museo Storico Navale

Easily the best city museum for children, this three-floor haven of shipbuilding includes Chinese junks and exhibits from World War II, such as the famed torpedoes guided by Italian Navy divers, responsible for sinking British warships (see p55).

6 Peggy Guggenheim Collection

Every Sunday the museum hosts Art4Family, free educational work-shops in English and Italian, run by artists and students from the Venice Academy of Fine Arts, for children aged 4 to 10 and their parents. You must book in advance (see pp40–41).

7 Lanterna Magica

MAP K5 ■ Campo San Barnaba, Dorsoduro 2808

Standing on a picture-postcard bridge, this delightful toy emporium caters for kids both young and old. Owners Marco and Francesco are veteran game designers specializing in Tolkien-related board games, making this a prime destination for gamer geeks.

8 Doge's Palace Prisons and Armoury

Children are thrilled by the spooky labyrinth of narrow passageways through the palace's erstwhile prisons, and it's fun deciphering the graffiti scratched on the walls by inmates over the centuries. In the armoury, hunt out the unusual child-sized suit from the 16th century, along with the protection for horses (see pp16–19).

9 Mistero e Magia

MAP R4 ■ Ruga Giuffa, Castello 4925

Run by a real magician, this shop is full of essentials such as wands, hats, and books revealing the tricks of the trade in Italian and English.

10 Visiting the Lido

If younger children are starting to tire of the galleries and museums, take them to play at the Lido. The free beaches offer hours of fun and not just in the summer. Bikes can also be hired (see pp122–5).

Beach at the Lido

🔟 Entertainment Venues

Stunning interior of Teatro La Fenice

③ Films in English
MAP M1 ▪ Videoteca Pasinetti: Salizzada San Stae, Santa Croce 1991 ▪ 041 524 13 20 ▪ www.comune.venezia.it ▪ Venice Film Festival: 041 521 87 11 ▪ www.labiennale.org

The Venice Film Library occasionally shows films in English during the winter. In late summer, the outdoor cinema in Campo San Polo shows some of the highlights from the Venice Film Festival.

① Teatro La Fenice
MAP N5 ▪ Tickets from Hello Venezia offices at the theatre (041 2424) or online ▪ www.teatrolafenice.it

World-famous opera and concert performances are held at this glorious theatre, re-inaugurated in December 2003 (see p81). Productions range from Verdi and Rossini to contemporary composers.

② Teatro Malibran
MAP Q2 ▪ Corte del Teatro Malibran, Cannaregio ▪ Tickets from Hello Venezia offices at the theatre (041 2424)

In a quiet square near Rialto stands the Malibran Theatre, re-inaugurated in 2001 to take on part of the Fenice's productions. Dating back to 1678 as Teatro Grimani, it was renamed after the 19th-century Spanish mezzo-soprano Maria Malibran.

Teatro Malibran

④ Teatro Goldoni
MAP P4 ▪ Calle del Teatro, S Marco 4650/B ▪ Ticket sales: 041 240 20 11 ▪ www.teatrostabileveneto.it

Teatro Goldoni is one of the oldest theatres in the city, dating from the 17th century. It acquired its present name in 1875 in honour of the 18th-century playwright Carlo Goldoni (see p46). An excellent range of international plays is performed in Italian between November and May.

⑤ Vivaldi Concerts
MAP Q4 ▪ Ateneo San Basso, Piazzetta dei Leoncini, San Marco ▪ 041 528 28 25 ▪ www.virtuosidivenezia.com

Inspiring, atmospheric performances of Vivaldi's music can be enjoyed in the intimate setting of Ateneo San Basso, which is just off Piazza San Marco. Tickets are available at agencies, hotels or directly from the palace.

⑥ Chamber Music
MAP M6 ▪ Campo S Vidal, S Marco 2862 ▪ 041 277 05 61 ▪ www.interpretiveneziani.com

While listening to the uplifting notes of Vivaldi's *Four Seasons* or a masterpiece from Bach or Benedetto Marcello, this is the perfect spot to take a moment to unwind and relax from the day's hectic sightseeing. The Church of San Vidal was rebuilt around 1700 and has a spacious interior.

Concerts in Costume
MAP J5 ■ Scuola Grande dei Carmini, Campo S Margherita, Dorsoduro ■ 041 528 94 20
■ www.musicainmaschera.it

Talented young singers and musicians perform comic operas at the Scuola Grande dei Carmini *(see p38)*. It makes for a memorable evening.

⑧ Venezia The Show
MAP P5 ■ Campo S Gallo, S Marco 1097 ■ 041 241 19 43
■ www.teatrosangallo.net

This is a highly entertaining and educational show celebrating the story of Venice. They also offer a dinner and show package.

⑨ Auditorium Santa Margherita
MAP K5 ■ Campo S Margherita, Dorsoduro 3689

This converted church *(see p38)* sometimes stages world and other music performances for free. Details are generally posted on the door.

Teatro Fondamenta Nuove

⑩ Teatro Fondamenta Nuove
MAP E2 ■ Fondamente Nuove, Cannaregio 5013 ■ 041 522 44 98
■ www.teatrofondamentanuove.it

Formerly a lumber store, since 1993 the premises have been buzzing with innovative theatre and contemporary dance. Experimental jazz music and offbeat films are also on the avant-garde programme.

TOP 10 FILMS SET IN VENICE

Indiana Jones in Venice

1 Summertime (1955)
Single American woman Katharine Hepburn meets an Italian man in Piazza San Marco and falls in love.

2 Indiana Jones and the Last Crusade (1989)
Hero Harrison Ford heaves up the floor in the church of San Barnaba.

3 Death in Venice (1971)
Visconti's film starring Dirk Bogarde is now as classic as the Thomas Mann novel on which it is based *(see p47)*.

4 Don't Look Now (1973)
This thriller, directed by Nicolas Roeg, with Donald Sutherland and Julie Christie, will keep you awake at night.

5 The Merchant of Venice (2004)
Shakespeare adaptation starring Al Pacino as a brilliant Shylock.

6 Eve (1962)
Joseph Losey's black-and-white classic starring "temptress" Jeanne Moreau.

7 Senso (1954)
Alida Valli betrays family and country for an Austrian officer in another Visconti film.

8 Fellini's Casanova (1976)
Donald Sutherland walks around a fantasized version of Venice in this Fellini film.

9 The Wings of the Dove (1997)
Helena Bonham Carter stars in the film version of Henry James's Venetian story.

10 Casino Royale (2006)
In his first outing as James Bond, Daniel Craig runs the city's alleys and makes a splash in the waterways.

Places to Eat in Venice

① Hotel Cipriani
MAP E6 ▪ Giudecca 10 ▪ 041 520 77 44 ▪ Closed Nov–Mar ▪ €€€

Guests are ferried from Piazza San Marco to this hotel restaurant, in a private launch, for a memorable gastronomic experience at two venues – Oro and Cip's Club. The former affords stunning views of the lagoon, and the latter offers fantastic views of St Mark's Square. One speciality is *tagliolini gratinati al prosciutto* (ribbon pasta with ham, browned in the oven).

Quiet, canal-side dining at Da Fiore

② Da Fiore
MAP M3 ▪ Calle del Scaleter, S Polo 2202/A ▪ 041 721 308 ▪ Closed Mon, 3 weeks in Jan, Aug ▪ No disabled access ▪ €€€

Reservations are essential at this sophisticated restaurant, where the owners base the day's menu on what is fresh at the market. They might have *pappardelle con ostriche e zafferano* (flat ribbon pasta with oysters and saffron) or *moleche fritte con polenta* (fried soft-shelled crab with polenta).

③ Grand Canal, Hotel Monaco
MAP Q6 ▪ Calle Vallaresso, S Marco 1325 ▪ 041 520 02 11 ▪ €€€

Traditional Venetian and Italian cuisine of a very high standard, including freshly made pasta with shrimp or seafood risotto, accompanied by the best of European wines. The setting, a terrace looking on to the Grand Canal, is stunning.

④ Osteria Boccadoro
MAP E3 ▪ Campo Widman, Cannaregio 5405 ▪ 041 521 10 21 ▪ €€€

Delicate flavours and fresh ingredients feature in dishes such as ribbon pasta with scallops and courgette (zucchini) flowers. Beware the *mousse al cioccolato* – it's made with five different sorts of chocolate! Romantically situated beneath a vine-clad pergola.

⑤ Corte Sconta
MAP F4 ▪ Calle del Pestrin, Castello 3886 ▪ 041 522 70 24 ▪ Closed Sun & Mon, Jan, mid-Jul–mid-Aug ▪ €€€

This former *osteria* is now a trendy restaurant that serves memorable seafood in a pretty "hidden courtyard" *(corte sconta)*. Don't miss the *pincia*, the local bread pudding, for dessert. The house wine is also wonderful. Booking ahead is essential.

⑥ Do Forni
MAP Q4 ▪ Calle Specchieri, S Marco 468 ▪ 041 523 21 48 ▪ No disabled access ▪ €€€

Right by Piazza San Marco, frequented by business people and politicians. Customers enter an imitation Orient Express dining car to be greeted by displays of glistening seafood. Book ahead.

⑦ Vini da Gigio
MAP D2 ▪ Fondamenta S Felice, Cannaregio 3628/A ▪ 041 528 51 40 ▪ Closed Mon & Tue, 2 weeks in Aug ▪ No disabled access ▪ €€

Tiny restaurant with a great reputation. The owner prides himself on his Italian and foreign wines to accompany dishes such as *tagliata di tonno* (fresh tuna fillet with herbs). Booking is recommended.

8 La Bitta
MAP K6 ▪ Calle Lunga de San Barnaba, Dorsoduro 2753 ▪ 041 523 05 31 ▪ No credit cards ▪ Closed Sun ▪ Disabled access ▪ €€

A cosy, rustic restaurant specializing in succulent meat dishes. No fish on the menu. Superb wine selection.

9 Osteria di Santa Marina
MAP Q2 ▪ Campo S Marina, Castello 5911 ▪ 041 528 52 39 ▪ Closed Sun, Mon lunch, 2 weeks in Jan ▪ €€€

Seafood is the star of the menu at this elegant restaurant; the baby octopus with red onion and orange is highly recommended.

10 Trattoria alla Madonna
MAP P3 ▪ Calle della Madonna, S Polo 594 ▪ 041 522 38 24 ▪ Closed Wed, 3 weeks in Jan, 25 Dec–31 Jan ▪ No disabled access ▪ €€

Traditional restaurant with an inspiring display of fresh seafood: *spaghetti con nero* (with cuttlefish ink sauce) and *anguilla fritta* (fried eel). It is not possible to make a reservation, so expect to queue.

Trattoria alla Madonna

TOP 10 WHAT TO EAT

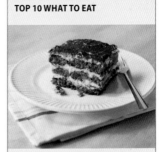

Tiramisù, a classic Italian dessert

1 Carpaccio
Raw beef sliced thin and sprinkled with rocket (*rucola*) or flakes of Parmesan cheese.

2 Sarde in Saor
Fried sardines marinated in a sweet-and-sour mixture of onions, currants and pine nuts, invented for sailors at sea for lengthy periods.

3 Antipasto di Frutti di Mare
Seafood platter of baby octopus, anchovies, shrimp or whatever else is in season.

4 Prosciutto e Melone
The sweetness of wedges of fresh rock melon is contrasted with the slightly salty cured Parma ham.

5 Risotto di Pesce
Clams, mussels, shrimp and assorted fish in a heavenly creamy rice dish.

6 Pasta con il Nero di Seppia
Usually spaghetti, combined with a rich sauce of tomato and cuttlefish, thoroughly blackened with the ink.

7 Fegato alla Veneziana
Venetian-style calves' liver cooked slowly with onions and vinegar.

8 Grilled Fish
Such as *coda di rospo* (monkfish) or *pesce spada* (swordfish) from the south.

9 Grilled Vegetables
Radicchio (red chicory) in winter, *zucchine* (courgettes) and *melanzane* (aubergine/eggplant) in summer, and roasted *peperoni* (peppers).

10 Tiramisù
Dessert with a creamy sauce of eggs and mascarpone between layers of sponge drenched in coffee or liqueur.

For a key to restaurant price ranges see p87

🔟 Osterie (Wine Bars)

Cantina Do Mori

1 Cantina Do Mori
MAP N2 ▪ Calle dei Do Mori, S Polo 429

Rows of copper polenta pots hang overhead in this dark, popular bar, billed as the city's oldest *osteria*. The affable owners pour wine directly from huge demijohns and serve delicate postage-stamp-sized ham and salad sandwiches *(francobolli)*.

2 Un Mondo diVino
MAP E3 ▪ Salizzada S Canciano, Cannaregio 5984A

Italian wines can be enjoyed at this converted butcher's shop, along with mouthwatering bar snacks such as *insalata di mare* (seafood salad) and regional cheeses. This place is well frequented by both locals and visitors, who spill out from the bar and into the alleyway, glass in hand.

3 Osteria Ruga Rialto
MAP N3 ▪ Ruga Vecchia S Giovanni, S Polo 692A

Verging on rowdy, this traditional establishment turns out crisp mounds of fried calamari and vegetables at evening *aperitivo* time, when you'll have to elbow your way past the locals to reach the bar. Lunch and dinner are somewhat quieter affairs.

4 Osteria del Sacro e Profano
MAP P2 ▪ Ramo secondo del Parangon, S Polo 502

Well worth hunting out near Rialto, this rustic-looking *osteria* is the haunt of international artists, who happily mingle with the locals. Wines from the Veneto and Friuli are served with traditional snacks such as *uova con acciughe* (hard-boiled egg with anchovy).

5 Vinus Venezia
MAP K4 ▪ Calle del Scalater Rocco, Dorsoduro 3961

This stylish wine bar serves a fantastic range of local and national wines, accompanied by elegant bar snacks made from locally produced ingredients, such as artichoke crostini.

6 Enoteca do Colonne
MAP C2 ▪ Rio Terrà del Cristo, Cannaregio 1814C

Animated neighbourhood bar with all manner of counter food ranging from *baccalà* (salted cod) on crusty bread to hearty *musetto* sausage, served with great smiles by the affable young owners. Decent selection of Veneto wines too.

Enoteca do Colonne

7 Osteria alla Frasca
MAP E2 ■ Corte della Carità, Cannaregio 5176

Billed as the site where Titian kept his paints and canvases, now this tiny picturesque bar serves drinks and snacks on a vine-covered terrace in summer.

8 Trattoria Antico Calice
MAP Q3 ■ Calle dei Stagneri, S Marco 5228

You have to fight your way through the locals here, attracted by the lively atmosphere and counter overflowing with local wines and appetizing snacks such as fried sardines in breadcrumbs.

9 Trattoria Ca' d'Oro alla Vedova
MAP D2 ■ Calle del Pistor, Cannaregio 3912

A young and enterprising new management team has taken over this timber-panelled establishment. This place has been serving up mouthwatering counter snacks (cicheti) such as crispy battered artichokes along with quaffable wine for longer than any of the regulars can remember.

Al Bottegon

10 Al Bottegon
MAP C5 ■ Fondamenta Nani, Dorsoduro 992

Not far from the Accademia Bridge, join the locals at this family-run specialist wine cellar that serves excellent Prosecco at the stand-up bar. Simple nibbles to accompany the wine include *mortadella* sausage and *panini* filled with *sopressa*, a local salami.

TOP 10 DRINKS

Refreshing Spritz al Bitter

1 Spritz
Unrivalled Venetian favourite of white wine with a splash of Bitter, Aperol or Select (*aperitivo* brands) and a shot of mineral water.

2 Prosecco
Excellent, naturally sparkling, dry white wine from the hills around Conegliano and Valdobbiadene.

3 Bellini
Smooth fresh peach juice and sparkling Prosecco blend, invented by Cipriani of Harry's Bar (*see p25*).

4 Red Wine
An *ombra* means a small glass of house wine, otherwise try quality Cabernet, Valpolicella or Amarone.

5 White Wine
Soave and Pinot Grigio are worthwhile alternatives to house varieties.

6 Mineral Water
Widely consumed in Italy, either sparkling (*con gas*) or still (*senza gas*). Tap water is *acqua dal rubinetto*.

7 Fruit Drinks
These can be ordered as *spremuta* (freshly squeezed juice) or *succo di frutta* (bottled nectars).

8 Coffee
Straight espresso, frothy cappuccino or *caffè latte* in a tall glass with hot milk.

9 Hot Chocolate
Usually served in the winter months. An *espresso* milk-free version can be found in good chocolate emporia.

10 After-dinner Sgroppino
A well-kept local secret concocted with lemon sorbet, vodka and Prosecco.

TOP10 Pubs, Bars and Clubs

Paradiso Perduto

1 Paradiso Perduto
MAP D2 ▪ Fondamenta della Misericordia, Cannaregio 2540
▪ 041 720 581

Call it animated or just plain noisy, but live world music, flowing wine and simple seafood are all part of the vibrant atmosphere at "Paradise Lost". Always packed full to the (low) rafters, the exuberant crowd often spills out onto the canal side where tables are set up in spring and summer months.

2 La Cantina
MAP N1 ▪ Campo San Felice, Cannaregio 3689 ▪ 041 522 82 58 ▪ Closed Sun

This bustling bar specializes in oysters shucked to order and other superbly fresh raw-fish delicacies. There is tasty charcuterie too, and an array of up to 30 wines to order by the glass. Elbow your way to the bar or grab an outside table.

3 The Irish Pub
MAP D2
▪ Campiello dei Testori, Cannaregio 3847
▪ 041 099 01 96

This is a marvellous pub with a lively Celtic atmosphere. You can always count on action here – a concert of Irish music in the cosy square, or screens showing rugby and football games. At Carnival and, of course, on St Patrick's Day, this is the place to be.

4 Bacaro Jazz
MAP Q3 ▪ Salizzada Fontego dei Tedeschi, S Marco 5546 ▪ 041 528 52 49

An enthusiastic multilingual welcome is extended to all visitors in this lively wine bar that never seems to close. It boasts almost non-stop service, an extended "happy hour" from 4 to 7pm and a delicious assortment of Spanish-style tapas snack meals to accompany the wine.

Bacaro Jazz

5 Skyline

MAP B6 ▪ Molino Stucky Hilton, Campo San Biagio, Giudecca 810 ▪ 041 272 33 11

This bar on the rooftop of the Molino Stucky Hilton hotel is the ultimate spot for a refreshing sundowner. Enjoy a cocktail as you gaze across the canal towards the Zattere, or take a dip in the pool.

6 Casinò Municipale, Palazzo Vendramin-Calergi

MAP C2 ▪ Campiello Vendramin, Cannaregio 2040

A magnificent start to an exciting evening – a special ACTV launch from Piazzale Roma transports hopeful clients down the Grand Canal to the landing stage of the beautiful Renaissance palace, alias City Casino, for a glittering night at the tables or the slot machines. It is also a short walk from the San Marcuola ferry stop.

7 Martini Scala-Club Piano Bar

MAP N5 ▪ Campo S Fantin, S Marco 1980 ▪ Closed Tue ▪ 041 522 41 21

This chic locale is the only place in Venice where you can enjoy high-quality cuisine and wine until the small hours of the morning, while being entertained by live music in air-conditioned comfort. No sleeveless tops or shorts, for men or women, are allowed.

8 Osteria da Filo

MAP L2 ▪ Calle del Tentor, Santa Croce 1539 ▪ 041 524 65 54

This relaxed bar is popular with students, who come for the cold-cut platters and the house wine, or to sip one of the many cocktails on offer. La Poppa, as it is fondly known, is open until 11pm every night.

9 Piccolo Mondo

MAP L6 ▪ Calle Contarini Corfù, Dorsoduro 1056/A ▪ 041 520 03 71

This tiny club, which does not open until 11pm, has a laid-back atmosphere. Entrance close to the Accademia Galleries.

10 Le Bistrot de Venise

MAP P4 ▪ Calle dei Fabbri, S Marco 4685 ▪ 041 523 66 51 ▪ Closed 22–25 Dec ▪ www.bistrotdevenise.com

An eclectic programme of events here never ceases to entertain, from poetry readings to art exhibitions and wine and food events. An added bonus is superb wine and a fascinating menu of dishes based on traditional 15th-century recipes.

Alfresco dining at Le Bistrot de Venise

Shops in Venice

① Ca' Macana
MAP K6 ▪ Calle delle Botteghe, Dorsoduro 3172

Buy one of Venice's famous papier-mâché masks at this shop, which carries the full Carnival range and much more besides. You can watch the mask-makers in action or even attend a course in making or painting your own.

② Nardi
MAP Q5 ▪ Piazza S Marco 69, S Marco

Elizabeth Taylor, Grace Kelly and Elton John have all happily spent time (and more) in this plush boutique of glittering marvels. Three generations of craftsmen have thrilled those who can afford it with breathtaking pieces, such as their blackamoor brooch in ruby and gold or diamond and platinum.

③ Luigi Bevilacqua
MAP L2 ▪ Campiello della Comare, S Croce 1320

Shimmering velvets, silks and damasks are fashioned into wonderful bags, clothes and shoes. The Bevilacqua family has been weaving precious fabrics by hand since the 1700s and you can see the ancient looms they continue to use today (see also p85).

Ancient looms at Luigi Bevilacqua

④ Venini
MAP Q4 ▪ Piazzetta Leoncini, S Marco 314

Don't expect Venetian glass animals here, rather innovative platters and vases of great simplicity and style. Since its 1921 beginnings, Venini's award-winning design team has included top names Carlo Scarpa and Gae Aulenti.

⑤ Attombri
MAP P3 ▪ Sottoportico degli Orefici, S Polo 65

Beautifully crafted bead jewellery is made on the premises by brothers Stefano and Daniele. Pieces range from delicate earrings to in-your-face flamboyant necklaces.

Colourful pasta at Rizzo

⑥ Rizzo
MAP Q2 ▪ Salizzada S Giovanni Crisostomo, Cannaregio 5778

Jet-black tagliatelle ribbons coloured with cuttlefish ink are just one option out of more than 40 imaginative pasta shapes that can be found on sale at Rizzo. Mouthwatering handmade chocolates and multicoloured Carnival masks also make marvellous souvenirs to take home.

⑦ Coin Department Store
MAP Q2 ▪ Salizzada S Giovanni Crisostomo, Cannaregio 5787

It's impossible to walk past the stylishly dressed windows of

Coin without being impressed. Centrally located close to the Rialto GPO, this branch of Italy's largest department chain has an elegant clothing range and sleekly designed homeware.

8 Rubelli
MAP M4 ■ Campiello del Teatro, S Marco 3877

Venice's past contact with the Orient is conjured up by the sumptuous handmade furnishings in this showroom. A blend of computer technology and traditional techniques is used for the brocades, damasks and silks.

Paolo Olbi

9 Paolo Olbi
MAP N4 ■ Dorsoduro 3253/A

This shop contains exquisite photo albums and address books in rainbow-coloured marbled paper and leather. All at reasonable prices, they are made by one of the original craftsmen in Venice.

10 Signor Blum
The meticulously hand-crafted and hand-painted wooden items on display in this corner store make for original presents and souvenirs. The range includes pictures of the city's landmark buildings and portraits of outstanding musicians as fridge magnets (*see p100*).

TOP 10 SOUVENIRS

Murano glassware

1 Glassware
Impress your guests back home with a genuine Murano chandelier or perhaps a *millefiori* paperweight.

2 Gourmet Food
For something authentically Italian but intrinsically Venetian, try extra virgin olive oil flavoured with chilli peppers, bottled red chicory paste or pasta in the shape of gondolas and masks.

3 T-shirts
The essential guaranteed souvenir of Venice, sold at the ubiquitous street stalls.

4 Masks
A mind-boggling array of masks, traditionally made for Carnival in papier-mâché, ceramic and even leather.

5 Marbled Paper
Swirls of pastel hues can be used for covering books or simply as elegant wrapping paper for gifts.

6 Beads
All manner of beads, from frosted glass to ceramic or the traditional, colourful murrhine mosaic-style, can be found.

7 Italian Wine and Liqueurs
Take advantage of lower prices and taxes by stocking up on locally produced wines.

8 Fabric
Lace is the most Venetian of materials, but attractive linens and velvets are also good value.

9 Silverwork
Photo frames, letter openers and teaspoons make lovely gifts for friends.

10 Clothes
All the top fashion names can be found in Venice.

🔟 Festivals and Events

① Carnival
Feb–Mar, concluding on Shrove Tue, 40 days before Easter

An unmissable 10-day extravaganza that takes over the city as a countdown to Lent. The streets mill with costumed and masked local "nobility" or crazily attired visitors. It gets off to a flying start with the Volo dell'Angelo (flight of the angel), when either an acrobat or a cardboard dove

Carnival-goer in full costume

is launched from the Campanile in Piazza San Marco, showering onlookers with confetti. The grand finale is the explosive Mardi Gras.

② Regata Storica
1st Sun in Sep

The word regatta originated in Venice, so what better place to enjoy the year's most spectacular event. Ornately decorated boats propelled by costumed oarsmen parade down the Grand Canal bearing passengers dressed as historical dignitaries. A series of furiously contested regattas follows.

③ Vogalonga
May: Sun after Ascension

A colourful armada of rowing craft from all over the world embarks on a 32-km (20-mile) non-competitive route around the lagoon's scattered islands. The "Long Row" is a great experience for both participants and onlookers, who line the Canale di Cannaregio towards midday to cheer on the breathtaking final stretch down the Grand Canal.

④ Festa del Redentore
Mid-Jul

People crowd on to all available watercraft, decorated with paper lanterns and greenery, for a feast of roast duck and watermelon, followed by a midnight fireworks display. It all takes place near Palladio's church on Giudecca (see p123) to commemorate the end of the 1576 plague. For those getting there on foot, a temporary pontoon bridge stretches from the Zattere over the Giudecca canal.

⑤ Biennale Art Exhibition
Jun–Nov

The world's leading international art bonanza is held on a two-yearly basis. The leafy gardens in eastern Castello are the principal venue, supplemented by the Corderie building in the Arsenale.

Colourful boats fill the Grand Canal for the Regata Storica

6 Festa della Salute
21 Nov

Venetians make a pilgrimage to Longhena's church *(see p52)* every winter in memory of the devastating plague of 1630–31. The whole area assumes a festive atmosphere with stalls selling candy floss and balloons.

Festa della Salute

7 Venice Marathon
Late Oct

Runners from all parts of the globe begin this classic – not to mention beautiful – 42-km (26-mile) race at Villa Pisani on the Brenta waterway, cross the causeway to Venice, the Zattere and San Marco, and finish near the public gardens in Castello.

8 Su e Zo per i Ponti
Late Mar/Apr: 4th Sun in Lent

Anyone can join this leisurely non-competitive walk or run "up and down the bridges". Several official routes can be followed, and all participants receive a medal on finishing.

9 Festa della Sensa
May: Ascension Day

Head for the Riviera di San Nicolò at the Lido *(see p123)* to watch this ancient ceremony of "Venice wedding to the Sea". A costumed "doge" casts a ring into the sea amid a procession of celebratory boats. Symbolizing Venice's maritime supremacy, La Sensa has been staged since Venice took Istria and Dalmatia in AD 997.

10 Festa di San Rocco
16 Aug

The feast day of St Roch, the French saint adopted by the confraternity for alleviating the 1576–7 plague, is celebrated each year at the Scuola Grande di San Rocco *(see p89)*.

TOP 10 SPORTS IN VENICE

A women's rowing team, practising on the waterways of Venice

1 Rowing
MAP D5 ▪ Zattere, Dorsoduro
Immensely popular Venetian pastime practised standing up. Join the oldest club, Canottieri Bucintoro.

2 Cycling
MAP H2 ▪ Gran Viale SM Elisabetta
Illegal in Venice itself, though you'll see kids zooming around. It is allowed in Lido, where you can rent a bike from a cycle shop on the main street.

3 Sailing
Yachtsmen gather at the marina on San Giorgio Maggiore island.

4 Swimming
Head for the Lido, or the crowded indoor pools at Sacca Fisola and Sant'Alvise.

5 In-Line Skating
There is a small rink at Sant'Elena in Castello, otherwise stick to the Lido pavements *(see p123)*.

6 Golf
MAP H2 ▪ Strada Vecchia, 1
The well-reputed 18-hole course at the Alberoni is on the south of the Lido.

7 Tennis
MAP H2 ▪ Lungomare G Marconi 41/D
The Lido has the only courts available to visitors.

8 Jogging
The city's stone paving doesn't do wonders for your knees, so try the city parks.

9 Gyms
Private gyms with state-of-the-art equipment can be found online.

10 Football
MAP H2 ▪ Stadio Pierluigi Penzo
The home team Venezia plays at Sant'Elena stadium on Sundays.

🔟 Venice for Free

Mosaics in the Basilica San Marco

1 Basilica San Marco

Entry to the city's main church, plastered with glittering Byzantine mosaics, is free of charge. Modelled on a mosque in Constantinople, the cavernous building has walls lined with artistically cut rock-slabs and superb geometric patterns on the floor (see pp12–13).

2 Take a Free Walking Tour

www.venicefreewalkingtour.com

Every morning and afternoon, free guided walking tours in English are organized from Campo Santi Apostoli in Cannaregio. Knowledgeable volunteers accompany visitors on short walks through places off the beaten track. It is essential to book ahead to ensure a place.

3 Art Night

www.artnightvenezia.it

Concerts, exhibitions, lectures, demonstrations of craft techniques, and videos are on all over the city on a set night in June (see the website), all organized by the City Council and Ca' Foscari University. Reservations are necessary for some events.

4 Free Museum Entry

On the first Sunday of each month, entry to all Italian state-run museums and galleries is free for all visitors. In Venice, this includes the Galerie dell'Accademia, Galeria Franchetti alla Ca' d'Oro, Museo Archeologico, Museo d'Arte Orientale and Palazzo Grimani.

5 Watching the Boats Go By

Settle down on any canal edge, and enjoy the unique sight of people going about their day-to-day business by boat – rubbish barges, transport floats, florist boats, taxi launches, to mention a few. And the water is often shared by ducks and cormorants fishing. Choice spots are Punta della Dogana (see p98), the Zattere (see p97) and the main Cannaregio canal.

6 Sala San Marco Biblioteca Museum of Medical Instruments

MAP R2 ■ Ospedale Civile, Campo SS Giovanni e Paolo, Castello ■ Open 9:30am–12:30pm, 2–5pm Tue–Sat

Above the entrance to Venice's public hospital (ospedale civile) with its marvellously ornate façade, this library is open to the public. Come here to marvel at the art work and grimace at the collection of historical surgical instruments.

7 Museo della Musica

MAP N6 ■ Chiesa di S Maurizio, Campo S Maurizio, S Marco ■ 041 241 18 40

This fascinating museum in converted church premises offers free entrance, allowing visitors to admire its historical collection of remarkable musical instruments dating back to the time of Vivaldi.

Museo della Musica

8 Isola di San Michele Cemetery

An island circled by tall brick walls and dotted with cypress trees houses the city's monumental cemetery (see p118). Even if you have little interest in paying homage at the tombs of notable residents Igor Stravinsky, Diaghilev or Joseph Brodsky, it's a pleasant spot simply for strolling around.

Isola di San Michele Cemetery

9 Castello Giardini Pubblici

Over in the Castello district, these gardens were laid out in the late 1800s by the French occupiers, as quickly becomes clear from the style. Shade and benches can be enjoyed to rest your weary feet, while the children let off steam in the playground (see p111).

Castello Giardini Pubblici

10 Free Concerts

In churches and neighbourhood halls, orchestras and choirs from Italy and overseas often hold concerts, which are free to spectators. To find out about these events in advance, check the street posters affixed to the city walls.

TOP 10 MONEY-SAVING TIPS

Avoiding café service charges

1 For cheap accommodation search for last-minute deals at online websites. Alternatively, use a hostel instead of a pricier hotel.

2 A house exchange is a low-cost way to experience Venice – and to live as the locals live.

3 Admire masterpieces – paintings and sculptures – in the city's many churches, where admission charges are modest.

4 Buy a slice of pizza at one of the many *pizza al taglio* establishments. It's the perfect food option when you're on the go.

5 Buy picnic supplies at a supermarket, and fill up your water bottle at a tap or fountain.

6 Purchase a Venezia Unica pass in advance online (www.veneziaunica.it). You can use this for ferries and sightseeing, saving both queuing time and money.

7 To avoid the waiter service charge at cafés, do as the locals do and take your drink at the bar instead of sitting down at a table.

8 During the Biennale art event (every two years; www.labiennale.org), visit the many free shows that are dotted around the city.

9 Cheap fashion clothes and shoes are on sale at the weekly markets on the Lido on Tuesday.

10 The Rolling Venice card (www.veneziaunica.it) offers discounted rates at shops and restaurants for young visitors (those aged 6–29).

📙 Frequently Asked Questions

A man wading through a flooded *fondamenta* in Cannaregio

① Is Venice still sinking?

Theoretically, that all came to a halt when the industries in Marghera stopped pumping out groundwater. However, studies have documented a rise in relative sea level, combined with accelerating subsidence due to changes in plate tectonics and soft sediments compacting under the weight of buildings.

② What do the buildings stand on?

During the course of the city's history, millions of pinewood piles from the Republic's carefully cultivated forests in the Alps were driven deep into the compressed clay-mud base and, over time, petrified in the absence of oxygen. These were successively overlaid with horizontal planks and marble-like Istrian stone slabs which served as the foundations for buildings.

③ Do people often fall in the water?

The odd tourist miscalculates the distance between the quayside and a waiting water taxi and takes the plunge – inevitably saved by timely intervention from a bystander. Be wary of moss-covered steps when taking a photograph or a rest and, of course, don't let young children out of your sight near water.

④ Why don't people restore the crumbling buildings?

Strict regulations concern façades – only porous stucco can be used for renovation as anything else tends to come away in sheets in damp, windy weather and is a hazard for passers-by. As a result, freshly plastered façades start crumbling weeks after application due to the high humidity and salt content in the air.

Crumbling canal-side buildings

THE MOSES FLOODGATES

The huge "Moses" dam project to protect Venice and its lagoon from exceptionally high flood tides entails the construction of massive hinged water-filled caissons fixed to the sea bed. These will be pumped empty and swung up to the surface to block off the lagoon entrances at Lido, Alberoni and Chioggia when needed.

The project is very controversial not only because of environmental concerns (upsetting the tidal flows in the lagoon ecosystem), but also due to recent corruption scandals involving the management.

5 How deep is the lagoon?

At its maximum depth, 15 m (49 ft) in the navigable channels dredged for shipping and marked out by the *bricole* poles. Concern about the danger of silting and obstruction of the city's lifeline waterways has always been high – one preventative measure was to reroute two rivers into the Adriatic Sea away from the lagoon. The Brenta was gradually modified between 1400 and 1600 to have it flow out after Chioggia, and the Sile was redirected towards Jesolo in the 1600s.

Boats line a back canal

6 Does everyone have a boat?

On summer Sundays you would be forgiven for thinking that is the case, as families pack small craft with picnic supplies, sunshades, fishing or stereo gear and row, sail, punt or speed out across the lagoon. Many, of course, need boats for work. On average, one in two families possesses a pleasure boat

7 How many people actually live in Venice?

In recent times, the population of Venice has fallen below the 60,000 mark, having shrunk by two-thirds since the 1950s. Moreover, this includes Italy's highest percentage of senior citizens. Venice's permanent population is experiencing a slow but inexorable decline as young couples prefer to move to the mainland with the convenience of a car, not to mention lower house prices, cheaper shopping and fewer tourists.

8 How does the house numbering system work?

Within each of the city's six administrative districts *(sestiere)*, numbers follow the alleyways along one side at a time, taking in branch streets and courtyards when encountered. In Cannaregio, the most extensive district, numbers reach 6420. The postmen are used to this confusing system, but visitors will need the name of the alley *(calle)*, square *(campo)* or quayside *(fondamenta)*.

9 Is the sea safe for swimming?

Yes. Periodic controls for bacterial counts are carried out and the upper Adriatic normally emerges with a clean slate. Venice's closest beach is at the Lido, where the city's families go en masse during the steamy summer months *(see p123)*.

10 Can you drink water from the drinking fountains?

Yes, it's the same as the tap water and subject to constant testing and treatment. Until 1884, when the supply piped from the mainland was inaugurated with a fountain in Piazza San Marco, the city depended on rainwater, which was meticulously drained and collected in cisterns beneath squares equipped with locked covered wells.

Public drinking fountain in a Venetian square

Venice
Area by Area

Lungo and Rio di San
Trovaso, Dorsoduro

𝗧𝗢𝗣 𝟭𝟬 San Marco

Venice's smallest but foremost *sestiere* (district), named after the city's patron saint, is bounded by the Grand Canal on all but one side, which explains the number of stately palaces in the area. It revolves around Piazza San Marco and the majestic Doge's Palace (*see pp16–19*), the political and legal core of the city until the 18th century. Running off the square are the Mercerie and Calle Larga XXII Marzo, offering wall-to-wall designer shopping. But beyond that San Marco has a residential air, with a great range of places to eat. Don't hesitate to wander down minor alleyways: surprises include unusual wellheads and many craft workshops.

Niccolò Tommaseo

AREA MAP OF SAN MARCO

- 1 Top 10 Sights
  see pp81–83
- 1 Places to Eat
  see p87
- 1 Craft Shops
  see p85
- 1 Bars and Cafés
  see p86
- 1 Designer Boutiques
  see p84

1 Piazza San Marco
See pp20–23.

2 Mercerie
MAP Q4

The expensive elegance of Venice is most evident on this main thorough-fare linking Rialto and Piazza San Marco. *Mercerie* means haber-dasher's, but these days it is home to designer fashion outlets. Just below the ornate Torre dell'Orologio archway is a sculpted female figure commemorating a housewife who lived here rent-free as a reward for inadvertently knocking a mortar into the street, killing a revolutionary leader and so halting the short-lived Bajamonte Tiepolo revolt in 1310.

3 Campo Santo Stefano
MAP M5

This spacious square is edged by cafés with smart, white-jacketed waiters and colourful awnings. Its most regular inhabitants seem to be unhurried pigeons, pecking around the ornate lampposts, and local children at play watched over by nannies and doting grandparents. Pride of place in the centre goes to a statue of Niccolò Tommaseo, patriot and author of the *Risorgimento*. At Carnival time a lively outdoor craft market is held here, although it is not quite up to the level of merry-making seen here in olden times, when there were magnificent balls and bullfights. The latter events ended in 1802 when a stand collapsed on spectators.

4 Teatro La Fenice
MAP N5 ■ **Campo S Fantin**
■ **Daily guided tours**

Long masked in scaffolding since a 1996 arson attack left it gutted, the historic "Phoenix" theatre rose from the flames in 2003. Selva's 1792 opera house has staged countless world premieres including Rossini's *Tancredi* in 1813, five operas com-missioned of Verdi, most notably *Rigoletto* and *La Traviata*, and works by Stravinsky and Luigi Nono. Legendary divas such as Maria Callas and Dame Joan Sutherland have sung in this glorious setting *(see p62)*.

Concert at Teatro La Fenice

5 Scala Contarini del Bovolo

MAP P4 ■ Corte dei Risi, S Marco 4299 ■ **Closed for restoration**

Often used as a film set, this fine 15th-century palace with its beautiful external "snail-shell" staircase (*bovolo* means snail in Venetian) is squeezed into a diminutive square deep in San Marco. The staircase is currently being restored. When it reopens, visitors will once again be able to climb the winding steps via five floors of loggias to a dome sheltering a splendid belvedere and enjoy magical panoramic views over the city's rooftops.

GLASSMAKING

Venetian glasswork exquisitely decorates chandeliers, chalices and mirrors and has long been in demand the world over, especially during the Golden Age of the 16th century. Although the industry moved to Murano (**above**) in 1295 as a safety measure against fire, there are still many furnaces around the San Marco district that welcome visitors.

6 Campo San Bartolomeo

MAP P3

The statue of celebrated Venetian playwright Carlo Goldoni scrutinizes the milling crowds on this crossroads square. Strategically placed for a host of inviting bars crammed into the alleys radiating off it, "San Bartolo" serves as the fashionable hang-out for the city's young and trendy. The northern end is occupied by the main post office, once home to Venice's German community *(see p45)*. They worshipped in the Chiesa di San Bartolomeo (open 10am–noon Tue, Thu & Sat; free admission).

Carlo Goldoni

7 Chiesa di San Moisè

MAP P5 ■ Campo S Moisè, S Marco 4299 ■ Open 9:30am–12:30pm Mon–Sat

So overloaded was the 1668 façade of this church with ostentatious Baroque stone decorations that several statues were removed in 1878 to save it from collapse. It has been blasted by critics as "the height of architectural folly" and by John Ruskin *(see p46)* as "one of the basest examples of the basest school of the Renaissance". Devoid of religious symbols, it is given over wholly to the glorification of the aristocratic Fini family, who laid out 30,000 ducats for the job.

8 Palazzo Grassi

MAP L5 ■ Campo S Samuele, S Marco 3231 ■ Open 10am–7pm Wed–Mon ■ Admission charge **(includes Punta della Dogana)** ■ www.palazzograssi.it

Set on the Grand Canal, the palace *(see p54)* dates back to 1740 when a wealthy merchant family commissioned Giorgio Massari to design the building. It is now home to the François Pinault collection, with contemporary masterpieces by Koons, Hirst and Pistoletto. It stands alongside picturesque Campo San Samuele, which features a graceful Veneto-Byzantine bell tower.

9 Museo Fortuny

MAP N4 ■ Campo S Benedetto, S Marco 3780 ■ Open 10am–6pm Wed–Mon ■ Admission charge ■ www.visitmuve.it

Flamboyant Spanish artist and theatrical stage designer Mariano Fortuny y Madrazo (1871–1950) adopted Venice as his home and muse, and transformed this 15th-century palace in

Gothic-Venetian style into an exotic atelier. The building retains rooms created by Fortuny himself and visitors can admire Fortuny's gorgeous velvets, his famous pleated silk dresses, paintings, lamps, a remarkable stage curtain and fascinating 19th-century photographs. The museum also hosts temporary exhibitions.

Museo Fortuny

⑩ Chiesa di Santa Maria del Giglio

MAP N6 ■ Campo S Maria del Giglio, S Marco 3231 ■ Open 10am–5pm Mon–Sat ■ Admission charge ■ www.chorusvenezia.org

Opening on to a lovely square next to the Grand Canal, this church is a further example of Venetian Baroque extravagance. Commissioned by the Barbaro family, its façade exalts their generations of maritime and political triumphs, with crests, galleys and statues. Works of art inside the church include Venice's only canvas by Rubens, depicting a Madonna and child. Tintoretto's contributions are the Evangelists on the organ doors.

Ceiling fresco in the Chiesa di Santa Maria del Giglio

A DAY IN SAN MARCO

▶ MORNING

Visit the **Doge's Palace** on Piazza San Marco first (see pp16–19), arriving early to fit it all in. Must-sees are the Sala del Senato, Sala del Maggior Consiglio, prisons and the Bridge of Sighs. Then take a break for coffee in the modern café in the palace's former stables and watch the gondolas glide past the glassed-in doorway.

Time your visit to **Basilica San Marco** (see pp12–15) for midday, to catch the mosaics illuminated by huge spotlights so they glitter to their utmost. The tiles were laid at angles to catch the light.

Lunch at **Harry's Bar**, as Hemingway's hero did in Across the River and into the Trees. Order the carpaccio (wafer-thin slices of raw beef) invented here by Cipriani (see p25).

AFTERNOON

The **Mercerie** (see p81) is shopper's heaven, packed with international high-fashion stores from Benetton to Cartier, and classy souvenir glass and hand-crafted paper workshops. For yet more, cross over to **Calle Larga XXII Marzo** for designer delights such as **Bulgari** and **Cartier** jewellery (see p84).

Return to **Piazza San Marco** (see pp20–23) in time to enjoy the views over Venice and the lagoon from the Campanile at dusk. At ground level again, it's time for a Bellini aperitivo at **Caffè Florian** (see p21) to watch the sun set over the façade of the basilica.

See map on pp80–81

Designer Boutiques

① Frette
MAP P5 ▪ Frezzeria,
S Marco 1725
Since 1860, Frette has been
importing top-grade cotton from
Egypt and transforming it into towels
and custom-made household linen.

L'Isola – Carlo Moretti

② L'Isola – Carlo Moretti
MAP M5 ▪ Calle delle
Botteghe, S Marco 2970
Contemporary glass at its most
innovative, exhibited in galleries all
over the world. Moretti's trademarks
are "paper cone" vases, tumblers
and huge sculptures.

③ Marina e Susanna Sent
MAP P5 ▪ Ponte S Moisè,
S Marco 2090
Come here for strikingly simple but
exquisitely elegant necklaces and
earrings in clear and coloured glass
designed by two sisters.

④ Ottico Fabbricatore
MAP P3 ▪ Calle dell'Ovo,
S Marco 4773
This small store offers an
array of exclusive
designer glasses with
frames made from
buffalo horn and
titanium, as well as
blown-glass vases
and lamps. You can also
get cashmere clothing in
70 colours and luxury
bags in various leathers.

⑤ Cartier
MAP P5 ▪ Calle San Moisè,
S Marco 1474
World-famous French jewellers
whose fortress-like premises gleam
with gold, precious stones and well-
crafted handbags and watches.

⑥ MaxMara
MAP P3 ▪ Campo S Salvador,
S Marco 5033
This family company has been
designing fashionable clothes and
accessories for city girls since 1951.

⑦ Bulgari
MAP P5 ▪ Calle Larga XXII
Marzo, S Marco 2282
Striking contemporary jewellery,
watches, accessories and Rosenthal
porcelain are sold here.

⑧ Fratelli Rossetti
MAP P3 ▪ Campo S Salvador,
S Marco 4800
This family-run firm was established
in 1953 and is known worldwide
for the superb Italian elegance it
displays in the likes of shoes, belts,
bags and jackets.

⑨ Fendi
MAP P5 ▪ Frezzeria,
S Marco 1582
Go straight to the source for
flamboyant frocks and shoes for
special occasions and crazily
beaded bags, all sporting the
"double-F" Fendi mark.

**Arnoldo e Battois
shoulder bag**

**⑩ Arnoldo
e Battois**
MAP P4 ▪ Calle
dei Fuseri, S
Marco 4271
Fabulous Italian
fashion is available
here from designers
Silvano Arnoldo and
Massimiliano Battois – let
them help you create your
look in this minimalist
cube of a store.

Craft Shops

1 **Venetia Studium**
MAP P5 ■ Calle
Larga XXII Marzo,
S Marco 2425
Exquisite hanging silk
lamps of Fortuny design
are reproduced with hand-
painted patterning and
glass beading.

2 **Legatoria Piazzesi**
MAP N6 ■ Campiello
della Feltrina, S Marco 2511
These are the only people in
Venice still printing paper
with hand-cut blocks, as
well as binding books.

3 **Pagnacco**
MAP Q4 ■
Mercerie, S Marco 231
Polar bears, kangaroos and
squirrels are but some of the
200 glass animals this wonderful
shop boasts. The shop window
is filled with orchestras of tiny
glass musicians.

4 **Leon d'Oro**
MAP P5 ■ Frezzeria,
S Marco 1770
Commedia dell'arte marionettes,
musical puppet theatres and
glittering Carnival masks are
available here for sale or hire.

5 **Galleria Livio De Marchi**
MAP M5 ■ Salizzada
S Samuele, S Marco 3157/A
Crumpled boots and a raincoat slung
over a chair are actually sculptures –
there are even life-size wooden cars,
complete with engines.

6 **Rigattieri**
MAP M5 ■ Calle dei Frati,
S Marco 3532/36
Ceramic enthusiasts must not miss
this extraordinary shop of beautiful
pottery. It has been run by the same
family since it was founded – at this
address – in 1938, and the focus is
firmly on high-quality goods.

Venetia Studium copper-
leaf free-standing lamp

7 **Valese Fonditore**
MAP Q4 ■ Calle
Fiubera, S Marco 793
The Valese family foundry
has been creating their
animals, lamps and door
knockers in brass and bronze
since 1913. Examples of their
work can even be found in
Buckingham Palace and The
White House.

8 **Le Botteghe
della Solidarità**
MAP P3 ■ Salizzada Pio X,
S Marco 5164
A kaleidoscopic display
of handwoven shawls
from India and musical
instruments from
African countries are
part of an enterprise that is intended
to guarantee artisans a just income.

9 **Bevilacqua**
MAP N5 ■ Campo S Maria
del Giglio, S Marco 2520
Small branch of this historic Italian
fabric shop. Handmade velvet and
silk cushions and tapestries are a
feast for the eyes *(see also p70)*.

Bevilacqua fabric shop

10 **Daniela Ghezzo
Segalin a Venezia**
MAP P4 ■ Calle dei Fuseri,
S Marco 4365
In addition to the brocade slippers
and bizarre footwear with built-in
toes, special-order shoes are also
hand-crafted here.

See map on pp80–81

Bars and Cafés

① Pasticceria Marchini Time

MAP P4 ▪ Campo S Luca, S Marco 4589

A paradise for those with a sweet tooth, Marchini is one of the oldest *pasticcerie* in the city. Orange and pistachio chocolates come in Venetian mask shapes.

② I Rusteghi

MAP Q3 ▪ Corte del Tintor, S Marco 5513 ▪ Closed Sun

Tucked away behind Campo San Bartolomeo, this is a cosy *osteria* run by a friendly sommelier-owner. Excellent selection of wines and *cicheti* (bar snacks).

③ Caffè Brasilia

MAP N4 ▪ Calle dei Assassini, S Marco 3658

Tuck into a huge, fresh fruit salad smothered with yogurt or a *tramezzino* (sandwich) in this quiet side-alley café, with tables inside and a few outside. The coffee's good, too.

④ Bar al Teatro

MAP N5 ▪ Campo S Fantin, S Marco 1916

Next door to the renowned Fenice Theatre (*see p81*), this legendary establishment offers outdoor seating on a patio. Otherwise go inside to the bar and munch a toasted sandwich.

Bar al Teatro

⑤ Devil's Forest Pub

MAP Q3 ▪ Calle dei Stagneri, S Marco 5185

This "English pub" sports a real red London phone box, draught beers and ales, and light meals that are served until midnight. There is even a dartboard and live music.

⑥ Bacarando

MAP P3 ▪ Corte dell'Orso, S Marco 5495

This great spot offers bar snacks at *aperitivo* time, but also has an elegant restaurant. Wednesday nights see the addition of live music.

Lime cocktail at Bacarando

⑦ Caffetteria Doria

MAP P4 ▪ Calle dei Fabbri, S Marco 4578/C

This is a friendly, standing-only corner bar serving divinely rich hot chocolate that is perfect for winter, and refreshing *sorbetto al caffè* in the summer months. There is also an impressive choice of teas.

⑧ Le Café

MAP M5 ▪ Campo S Stefano, S Marco 2797

Have a fresh orange juice or cappuccino and pastry as you watch life go by in the square. The usual hot dishes are available, and there is also a *pasticceria* offering tasty tarts and pastries.

⑨ Rosa Salva

MAP Q4 ▪ Ponte Ferai, S Marco 951

Come here to enjoy melt-in-the-mouth fruit tarts, exquisite pastries and Venice's best panettone.

⑩ Bar all'Angolo

MAP M5 ▪ Campo Santo Stefano, S Marco 3464

Tourists and locals alike are unable to resist this great sandwich bar. Bag a table outside for a well-earned coffee or light lunch.

Places to Eat

PRICE CATEGORIES
For a three-course meal for one with half a bottle of wine (or equivalent meal), taxes and extra charges.
....
€ under €40   €€ €40–60   €€€ over €60

1 Ristorante A Beccafico
MAP M5 ■ Campo S Stefano, S Marco 2801 ■ 041 527 48 79 ■ €€€
Marvellous southern Italian eatery. The menu includes pasta, meat and fish, plus fabulous desserts.

2 Ristorante alla Borsa
MAP N6 ■ Calle delle Veste, S Marco 2018 ■ 041 523 54 34 ■ €€€
A great selection of wines accompany dishes such as clams, mussels, tomatoes and capers.

3 Rossopomodoro
MAP Q4 ■ Calle Larga S Marco, S Marco 403 ■ 041 243 89 49 ■ €
Part of a popular pasta chain, Rossopomodoro prepares its authentic Neapolitan pizzas in a wood-burning oven.

4 Rosticceria San Bartolomeo
MAP P3 ■ Calle della Bissa, S Marco 5424 ■ 041 522 35 69 ■ No disabled access ■ €
Also known as the Gislon, this place serves great *mozzarella in carozza*, a deep-fried cheese sandwich.

5 Ai Assassini
MAP N4 ■ Rio Terrà dei Assassini, S Marco 2695 ■ 041 528 79 86 ■ Closed Sun ■ €€
Try the bar snacks or treat yourself to a table at this great *osteria* ideally situated near La Fenice *(see p81)*.

6 Leon Bianco
MAP P4 ■ Campo S Luca, S Marco 4153 ■ 041 522 11 80 ■ Closed Sat & Sun ■ €
Leon Bianco is a great spot for grilled meats and fish or lasagne.

You have the choice of eating at the bar or at a table outside. American Express not accepted.

7 Al Bacareto
MAP M5 ■ Calle delle Botteghe, S Marco 3447 ■ 041 528 93 36 ■ Closed Sun, Aug ■ €
A Venetian stalwart since 1971. Try the *bigoli in salsa* (spaghetti with anchovy and onion purée).

8 Osteria San Marco
MAP P5 ■ Frezzeria, S Marco 1610 ■ 041 528 52 42 ■ Closed Sun ■ €€
An exemplary wine list accompanies the tasty bar snacks and a small, but perfectly formed, menu.

9 La Caravella
MAP P5 ■ Via XXII Marzo, S Marco 2398 ■ 041 520 89 01 ■ No disabled access ■ €€€
Resembles a caravel sailing ship. Trestle tables are adorned with pewter plates, and fish and meat dishes are served. Good wine list.

La Caravella

10 Acqua Pazza
MAP N5 ■ Campo Sant'Angelo, S Marco 3808/10 ■ 041 277 06 88 ■ Closed Mon, 7 Jan–7 Feb ■ No disabled access ■ €€€
Mediterranean cuisine, including Neapolitan-style pizza.

See map on pp80–81 ←

📕TOP10 San Polo and Santa Croce

Venice's greatest concentration of sights can be found in these neighbouring districts, at the geographical heart of Venice, having grown around the ancient core of Rialto where the first inhabitants settled. Here, glorious churches, landmark monuments and breathtaking palaces are all saturated in history. Essential sights include Santa Maria Gloriosa dei Frari *(see pp32–3)*, the Scuola Grande di San Rocco, where Tintoretto demonstrated his genius on sumptuous canvases, and the morning bustle of Rialto market. The squares of San Polo and San Giacomo dell'Orio are both full of cafés and benches for resting weary feet.

Campo San Giacomo dell'Orio

AREA MAP OF SAN POLO AND SANTA CROCE

1 The Rialto
See pp34–5.

2 Campo San Polo
MAP M3

This lovely square undergoes a series of transformations, from attractive theatre or dance area during Carnival, to open-air cinema through the summer months, and playground for bicycle- and scooter-mad kids the rest of the year. It has never been particularly quiet – it was once a venue for bullfights and bird-netting, extravagant parties with fireworks displays and even crime. In 1548, Florentine writer-in-hiding Lorenzino de' Medici was stabbed to death here on orders from the great Cosimo de' Medici. It was punishment for the assassination of Cosimo's cousin, Duke Alessandro, which brought the Medici line to an end.

Scuola Grande di San Rocco

3 Scuola Grande di San Rocco
MAP K4 ■ Campo S Rocco, S Polo 3052 ■ Open 9:30am–5:30pm daily ■ Closed 1 Jan, 25 Dec ■ Admission charge ■ www.scuolagrande sanrocco.it

Blinding in the morning sun, the early Renaissance façade of this historic building, home to master-pieces by Tintoretto, is a marvel of intertwined sculpted stone wreaths and crouching elephants dwarfed by stately columns. The Istrian stone facing is embedded with a medley of burgundy porphyry and green- and cream-veined marble inserts. Designed by Bartolomeo Bon in 1517 and added to by Scarpagnino among others, the imposing building with neighbouring church was home to one of the city's foremost confraternities, honoured with an annual visit by the doge.

4 Campo San Giacomo dell'Orio
MAP L2

This quintessential picturesque square, well off the beaten track, sports plane trees, benches for relaxing and patches of grass. Modest surrounding palaces are home to Venice University's archi-tectural faculties. The laid-back air and abundance of eateries and coffee shops make it very inviting, and there's no lack of subjects for photographers or artists.

5 Chiesa di San Giacomo dall'Orio

MAP L2 ■ Campo S Giacomo dell' Orio, S Croce ■ Open 10am–5pm Mon–Sat ■ 041 275 04 62 ■ **Admission charge** ■ www.chorusvenezia.org

Do not miss this unusual church. Founded in the 9th century, its Latin-cross shape boasts a marvellous 15th-century wood-beamed ceiling and a forest of colourful granite and black limestone columns from the Middle East, several of them loot from the Crusades. The floor merits close scrutiny for its multitude of fossils, while memorable paintings include Palma il Giovane's *Descent of Manna* (1580–81), left of the main altar, and a painted crucifix (1350) attributed to Paolo Veneziano.

6 Scuola Grande di San Giovanni Evangelista

MAP L3 ■ Campiello della Scuola, S Polo 2454 ■ Open daily (times vary) ■ 041 71 82 34 ■ **Admission charge** ■ www.scuolasangiovanni.it

This erstwhile confraternity head-quarters with a high-ceilinged upstairs hall is mostly used for conferences. The monumental staircase was the work of Coducci and the priceless reliquary contains a fragment of the True Cross, presented to the Scuola in 1369. The spectacular *Miracles of the Cross* cycle of paintings commissioned by Gentile Bellini and associates is now in the Accademia Galleries (see pp30–31). The exterior courtyard has a fine sculptured portal screen by Pietro Lombardo mounted with an eagle to symbolize St John.

Scuola Grande di San Giovanni Evangelista

Palazzo Mocenigo

7 Palazzo Mocenigo

MAP M2 ■ Salizzada S Stae, S Croce 1992 ■ Open Apr–Oct: 10am–5pm Tue–Sun (to 4pm Nov–Mar) ■ Closed 1 Jan, 1 May, 25 Dec ■ 041 72 17 98 ■ **Admission charge** ■ www.visitmuve.it

An 18th-century patrician palace whose richly furnished and frescoed rooms have showcases of historic fabrics and costumes, plus a fascinating history of perfumes. The Mocenigo family portrait gallery has a total of seven doges, topped in fame by Alvise I, the victor at the 1571 Battle of Lepanto against the Turks, which was crucial for the Republic.

8 Campo San Zan Degolà

MAP L1 ■ Chiesa di San Giovanni Decollato: open 10am–noon Mon–Sat

People usually hurry through this square en route to the bus terminal, oblivious to its quiet charm. Interest starts with the curious loggia on the western canal edge, then there's the attractive plain church named for San Giovanni Decollato or St John the Beheaded, depicted with flowing curly locks in a stone bas-relief on the southern wall. Inside the simple Veneto-Byzantine building are lovely 13th-century frescoes, an unusual survivor for damp old Venice.

9 Giardino Papadopoli
MAP J3

A leafy haven of twittering sparrows and flowerbeds close to Piazzale Roma and the car parks, these French-designed gardens date back to the 1800s when extravagant parties for the nobility were held here among exotic flowers and rare animals. Site of a demolished convent, it belonged to Corfu-born entrepreneurs, hence the Greek name. The public park was greatly reduced in size when the Rio Nuovo canal was excavated in 1932–3.

Giardino Papadopoli

10 Ca' Pesaro Museo di Arte Orientale
MAP N1 ■ Fondamenta Ca'Pesaro, S Croce 2076 ■ Open Apr–Oct: 10am–6pm Tue–Sun (to 5pm Nov–Mar) ■ Admission charge ■ www.visitmuve.it

This impressive Oriental Art Collection is an eclectic mix of 19th-century curiosities from all over the Far East. Exhibits include armour, porcelain and costumes, lacquerwork boxes and musical instruments. The museum is on the third floor, above the modern art gallery in Ca' Pesaro (see p24 & p55). A single ticket grants admission into the gallery and the museum.

A DAY IN SAN POLO

▶ MORNING

Drink your fill of Tintoretto's dynamic paintings at the **Scuola Grande di San Rocco** (see p89) before wandering east to **Campo San Polo** (see p89). Coffee is a must in the square, either at one of the local bars or at the attractive **Antica Birraria La Corte** (see p93).

It's not far from here to **Rialto Market** (see pp34–5) for late-morning bargains of fresh produce, often nearing half-price when stall-holders are in a hurry to shut up shop. If this has worked up an appetite, a Grand Canal-side lunch is worth consideration at this point. There is a string of eateries spread along the sun-blessed **Riva del Vin**, close to the foot of Rialto Bridge. Each displays live lobster and fish and have multilingual menus. In winter diners sit in see-through "tents" so that views of the canal and the procession of boats are ensured.

AFTERNOON

Head north and explore the craft and gift shops, lace, scarf and T-shirt stalls along Ruga Rialto and the old red-light area of **Rio Terrà Rampani** (see p58).

Try to end up in pretty **Campo San Giacomo dell'Orio** (see p89) for a pre-dinner drink at **Al Prosecco** wine bar (Campo S Giacomo dell'Orio, S Croce 1503 • 041 524 02 22 • Closed Sun). Ask for a glass of the fruity red Refosco from Friuli and *bocconcino con mortadella di cinghiale* (bite-sized roll with sliced wild boar).

See map on pp88–9 ←

Craft Shops

1 Gilberto Penzo
MAP M3 ■ **Calle Seconda dei Saoneri, S Polo 2681**

A visit to this workshop with beautiful wooden models of traditional Venetian boats is a real treat. Many crafts come in DIY kit form.

2 Mazzon le Borse
MAP L4 ■ **Campiello S Tomà, S Polo 2807**

Since 1963, Papa Piero has been making beautiful leather bags that last a lifetime. Luckily his daughter Marta is taking over the reins.

Hand-painting masks at Tragicomica

3 Tragicomica
MAP M4 ■ **Calle dei Nomboli, S Polo 2800**

The result of 20 years of creating elaborate papier-mâché and leather masks and brocade costumes for Carnival, as well as theatrical productions, can be appreciated in this spectacular craft shop, where staff explain the significance of pieces.

4 Rivoaltus
MAP P3 ■ **Ponte di Rialto, S Polo 11**

Beautiful hand-bound diaries and address books can be purchased from this tiny shop, which is situated right on the Rialto bridge.

5 Laberintho
MAP M2 ■ **Calle del Scaletier, S Polo 2236**

Two goldsmiths create contemporary jewellery pieces and replicas of antique rings. For a special souvenir, they will also make something tailored to your specifications.

6 Sabbie e Nebbie
MAP M4 ■ **Calle dei Nomboli, S Polo 2768/A**

Customers come to this tasteful boutique to purchase pottery, candles and other oddities from Japan and Italy.

7 Attombri
MAP P2 ■ **Sottoportego degli Orefici, S Polo 74**

In an old covered passageway that has long been home to the Rialto Market goldsmiths, you will find two designer brothers who make limited-edition jewellery.

8 Dinamo
MAP L3 ■ **Calle del Tagiapiera, S Polo 2599/A**

A mix of ceramics, designer wares and fabrics created by local and foreign artisans.

9 Margherita Rossetto Ceramica
MAP K2 ■ **Corte Canal, S Croce 659**

Eggcups, teapots and platters are some of the delightful hand-turned objects available here.

10 La Pedrera
MAP L3 ■ **Campo Sant'Agostin, S Polo 2279/B**

Handmade beads, photo frames and Murano glass creations.

Necklaces at La Pedrera

Places to Eat

Elegant dining area at Muro

1 La Zucca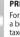
MAP L1 ■ Ponte del Megio, S Croce 1762 ■ 041 524 15 70 ■ Closed Sun ■ No disabled access ■ €€
Delicious vegetarian fare is served here, and there is also the promise of unforgettable chocolate desserts.

2 Osteria Banco Giro
MAP P2 ■ Campo S Giacometto, S Polo 122 ■ 041 523 20 61 ■ Closed Mon ■ €€
This is a trendy restaurant-bar along the Grand Canal serving a variety of quality Italian vintages and tasty nibbles.

Osteria Banco Giro

3 Al Nono Risorto
MAP N2 ■ Sottoportego de la Siora Bettina, S Croce 2337 ■ 041 524 11 69 ■ Closed Wed, Thu L ■ No credit cards ■ No disabled access ■ €
Lively eatery that serves great pizzas in the garden to a predominantly youthful clientele.

4 Il Refolo
MAP L2 ■ Campo San Giacomo dell'Orio, S Croce 1459 ■ 041 524 00 16 ■ Closed Mon, Tue L ■ €
Diners come to this great canal-side spot for inexpensive pizzas in a magical surrounding.

5 Osteria Mocenigo
MAP M1 ■ Salizzada San Stae, S Croce 1919 ■ 041 523 17 03 ■ Closed Mon ■ €
Don't miss the *cestino al parmiggiano*, a crisp fried pastry and cheese basket filled with prawns.

6 Muro
MAP N2 ■ Campiello dello Spezier, S Croce 2048 ■ 041 524 16 28 ■ No disabled access ■ €
Order steak or fish here – Antipasto Muro is a great seafood selection.

7 Antica Birraria La Corte
MAP M3 ■ Campo S Polo, S Polo 2168 ■ 041 275 05 70 ■ €
Delectable pizzas named after the city's bridges at this ultra-modern eatery set in a former brewery. There is also a tree-shaded patio.

8 Gelateria Alaska
MAP K2 ■ Calle Larga dei Bari, S Croce 1159 ■ €
Unforgettable ice cream made by a true maestro, Carlo. This is the real deal – 100 per cent natural gelato with ginger, spearmint, pistachio, rose petals or green tea.

9 Taverna Da Baffo
MAP L3 ■ Campo della Chiesa, S Polo 2346 ■ 041 520 88 62 ■ €
Seek out this tranquil square for a light lunch with a glass of Belgian beer or crisp Friuli wine.

10 Pasticceria Rizzardini
MAP M3 ■ Campiello dei Meloni, S Polo 1415 ■ Closed Tue, Aug ■ €
Neighbourly, old-style pastry shop serving thick hot chocolate and divine fruit tarts, almond slices and crunchy peanut toffee.

See map on pp88–9

TOP 10 Dorsoduro

A district of contrasts, Dorsoduro stretches from the port, via the panoramic Zattere and Grand Canal, all the way to the Punta della Dogana. Highlights for visitors include two foremost art galleries, the Accademia and the Peggy Guggenheim Collection *(see pp40–41)*, crammed with master-pieces ancient and modern, as well as Ca' Rezzonico palace *(see p50)* and magnificent churches, Santa Maria

Chiesa dei Gesuati, Zattere

della Salute *(see p52)* and San Sebastiano, the latter famous for its wonderful Veronese works. Literally the "hard backbone" of Venice built on elevated islands of compacted subsoil, Dorsoduro used to be sparsely populated. Today, as home to most of the city's university premises, it is full of lively cafés, bars and nightlife, concentrated in the market square, Campo Santa Margherita.

AREA MAP OF DORSODURO

① Top 10 Sights
see pp97–9

① Places to Eat
see p101

① Shops
see p100

Previous pages Basilica di Santa Maria della Salute, from the Campanile di San Marco

Accademia Galleries
See pp30–31.

Zattere
MAP C5

This broad waterfront took its name from the rafts of timber *(zattere)* floated downstream from the extensive forests in the northern Dolomite region which were managed by the Venetian Republic. The precious wood was either used for constructing palaces or transformed into masts and the like for the important shipbuilding industry. The tall-masted sailing ships and rowing boats that used to moor here have long since been replaced by motorized *vaporetti* and tourist launches, and nowadays the Zattere signifies lovely lagoon views and is perfect for a daytime or evening stroll.

San Nicolò dei Mendicoli
MAP A5 ■ Campo S Nicolò, Dorsoduro 1907 ■ 041 275 03 82 ■ Open 10am–noon, 3–5:30pm Mon–Sat, 9am–noon Sun

This Veneto-Byzantine church with an imposing square *campanile* (bell tower) is known to film buffs from Nicholas Roeg's chilling *Don't Look Now*. Hidden in a maze of narrow alleyways off the port zone, it has a pretty portico that doubled as a shelter for the poor. Founded in the 7th century, it is the second-oldest church in Venice. In the 1970s it was restored by the Venice in Peril Fund, who water-proofed the low floor.

San Nicolò dei Mendicoli

MASKS

Handmade in papier-mâché and glittery plaster, Venetian masks (**right**) are now strictly tourist fare, but they were once essential attire during Carnival, allowing aristocrats to enjoy themselves in anonymity. One unusual model, with a long curved nose, was used by doctors during plagues, its cavity filled with perfumed herbs to filter the diseased air.

4 Squero di San Trovaso
MAP C5

This is the city's most famous gondola repair and construction yard, though its days may be numbered. The combined workshop-dwelling is reminiscent of an Alpine chalet, as the first occupants came from the mountainous Cadore region. Closed to visitors, it backs on to a canal (Rio di San Trovaso), so it's easy to watch the caulking and cleaning in progress.

5 Chiesa di San Sebastiano
MAP B5 ▪ Campo S Sebastiano, Dorsoduro 1907 ▪ 041 275 04 62 ▪ Open 10am–5pm Mon–Sat ▪ Admission charge ▪ www.chorusvenezia.org

This 16th-century church is a treasure trove of Paolo Veronese paintings. The artist devoted most of his life to its fresco cycle (see p53).

6 Rio Terrà dei Catecumeni
MAP D5

A reclaimed thoroughfare between the Zattere and Santa Maria della Salute, this stretch is dominated by a long building, now a school, where prisoners-of-war of the Republic who did not profess the Christian faith were held captive until they converted. This quiet backwater comes alive on 21 November with the Salute festivities (see p73).

7 Ex Ospedale degli Incurabili
MAP C5 ▪ 423 Zattere, Dorsoduro 30135 ▪ Closed to public

A cavernous construction that takes up a lengthy stretch of the Zattere, this former hospital has undergone vast renovations to adapt it for the Accademia Art Institute, which was transferred here to leave the historic galleries room for expansion (see pp30–31). The building dates from the 1500s, founded to shelter women with incurable venereal diseases, and later took in orphans and also became a trade school. Legend has it that St Francis Xavier, ordained in Venice, was sent to serve here with his companions on orders from Ignatius Loyola. More recently, it has served as a juvenile court.

8 Punta della Dogana
MAP E5 ▪ Campo della Salute, Dorsoduro 2 ▪ 041 523 16 80 ▪ 10am–7pm Wed–Mon ▪ Admission charge ▪ www.palazzograssi.it

This exciting addition to the Venetian contemporary art scene is housed in an imposing 17th-century customs building, the interior of which was renovated by Japanese architect Tadao Ando. It contains important works, including pieces by British artists Rachel Whiteread and the Chapman Brothers, and offers fantastic views towards St Mark's, San Giorgio and the two main canals of Venice. Tickets also grant entry into the Palazzo Grassi (see p82).

Punta della Dogana

Altar in Chiesa dei Gesuati

⑨ Chiesa dei Gesuati

MAP C5 ▪ Fondamente delle Zattere, Dorsoduro 917 ▪ 041 275 06 42 ▪ Open 10am–5pm Mon–Sat ▪ Admission charge ▪ www.chorusvenezia.org

Set right on the Zattere waterfront close to the main ferry moorings, the Gesuati (also known as Santa Maria del Rosario) is often confused with the Gesuiti (Jesuit) establishment in Cannaregio. Taking over from a minor religious order, the Domenican friars had this church constructed in Classical style in 1726 by Giorgio Massari. Inside, the ceiling consists of three uplifting frescoes (1737–9) by Tiepolo *(see p48)*, considered among his best work, portraying St Dominic amid glorious angels in flight.

⑩ San Basilio Port Zone

MAP B5

The vast docks occupy a good part of the northwestern continuation of the Zattere waterfront, and are usually crowded with trucks and cars queueing up to board the ferries to Greece. The modern terminal also handles the increasing cruise liner traffic, whereas the former industrial structures, such as the cotton mill and cold stores, are being converted for use by Venice University. The outstanding 17th-century pastel portrait artist Rosalba Carriera was born in the San Basilio parish and returned there to die, destitute and totally blind, in 1757.

Campo Santa Margherita

Margaret DuChamp

Scuola Grande dei Carmini

Accademia Galleries

Accademia Foscarini

Punta della Dogana

Al Chioschetto

Zattere

Santa Maria della Salute

▶ MORNING

The **Accademia Galleries** *(see pp30–31)* can be overwhelming, so focus your visit on a selection of its masterpieces, but don't neglect the Carpaccios and Bellinis. After all that art, have a relaxing coffee watching the boats go by at **Snack Bar Accademia Foscarini** *(Rio Terrà Antonio Foscarini, Dorsoduro 878/C • 041 522 72 81 • Closed Tue)*, a magical spot right at the foot of Accademia Bridge.

Next, head off east for a leisurely stroll, past Longhena's work of art, the church of **Santa Maria della Salute** *(see pp52–3)*, to **Punta della Dogana**, a great spot for taking photos of Piazza San Marco. Turn back in the direction of the **Zattere** and Giudecca Canal. Lunch is recommended at **Al Chioschetto** *(Zattere, Dorsoduro 1406/A)*, a bar right on the water's edge.

AFTERNOON

Wander through to **Campo Santa Margherita** *(see pp38–9)* to the **Scuola Grande dei Carmini** to admire Tiepolo's canvases, then take time to admire the architectural curiosities of this fascinating square.

As sunset approaches waste no time in occupying a table for a Spritz *aperitivo* at the trendy bar **Margaret DuChamp** *(Campo S Margherita, Dorsoduro 3019 • 041 528 62 55 • Closed Tue)*. It's hard to better this as a place for people-watching, and an added bonus is the scent of jasmine that fills the air as night falls.

See map on pp96–7

Shops

1 **3856**
MAP K4 ▪ Calle San Pantalon, Dorsoduro 3749
A small but perfectly assembled selection of clothing and accessories. The mother-and-daughter team are friendly and helpful.

2 **BAC Art Studio**
MAP D5 ▪ Piscina del Forner, Dorsoduro 862
Attractive and affordable etchings and prints of Venice by artists Baruffaldi and Cadore. Buy them framed if desired.

3 **Totem-Il Canale Gallery**
MAP C5 ▪ Rio Terrà Antonio Foscarini, Dorsoduro 878/B
Bulky ancient beads, made with vitreous paste and once traded in Africa, are now precious antiques. Contemporary African wood artworks as well.

4 **Signor Blum**
MAP K5 ▪ Campo S Barnaba, Dorsoduro 2840
Detailed jigsaw models of Gothic palaces, flanked by wall panels and painted toy figures, all individually handmade by this co-operative of female artisans.

Signor Blum

5 **Augusto Mazzon**
MAP L5 ▪ Calle del Traghetto, Dorsoduro 2783
Everyone's Christmas tree needs one of the joyous gilded cherubs lovingly crafted by wood-carver and painter Danilo. He also makes picture frames and furniture.

6 **Officina Veneziana**
MAP K4 ▪ Campo S Pantalon, Dorsoduro 3701
A wonderful selection of Art Deco jewellery, Easter eggs, Christmas decorations and fine china.

7 **Perla Madre Design**
MAP K5 ▪ Calle delle Botteghe, Dorsoduro 3182
Colourful selection of glass bead jewellery made right in front of your eyes by designer Simona Iacovazzi.

Trendy design shop Madera

8 **Madera**
MAP K5 ▪ Campo S Barnaba, Dorsoduro 2762
Uber-cool design store with minimalist pieces in wood and glass, as well as gorgeous ceramics.

9 **Libreria Toletta**
MAP L6 ▪ Sacca della Toletta, Dorsoduro 1213
A popular bookstore that specializes in art and architecture, but also houses a great collection of guidebooks and novels in English.

10 **Arras**
MAP L5 ▪ Campiello Squelini, Dorsoduro 3235
This shop stocks original hand-woven fabrics, garments and bags in beautiful colours.

Places to Eat

1 Gelateria Nico
MAP C5
■ Zattere, Dorsoduro 922 ■ 041 522 52 93
■ Closed Thu ■ €

This spot is Venice's most renowned ice-cream parlour. The local favourite is *gianduiotto da passeggio* – hazelnut and chocolate ice cream smothered in whipped cream.

Gianduiotto da passeggio

2 La Piscina
MAP C5 ■ Zattere, Dorsoduro 780 ■ 041 520 64 66 ■ Closed Mon ■ €€

The restaurant, with a lovely canalside terrace, serves Mediterranean and Venetian cuisine, including a wide range of delicious vegetarian dishes.

3 Bar Abbazia
MAP D5 ■ Rio Terrà dei Catecumeni, Dorsoduro 128–129/A ■ 041 523 21 49 ■ €

Shaded by a leafy pergola, the outside tables are perfect for enjoying a quick sandwich.

4 Impronta Caffè
MAP K4 ■ Calle dei Preti, Dorsoduro 3815 ■ 041 275 03 86
■ Closed Sun ■ €

Affordable meals and long opening hours make this a local favourite.

5 La Rivista
MAP C5 ■ Rio Terrà Foscarini, Dorsoduro 979/A ■ 041 240 14 25
■ Closed Mon ■ €€

Innovative Italian cuisine is offered here, in relaxing, designer, modern surroundings. Inspiring choice of cheese and wines.

6 Ai Gondolieri
MAP D5 ■ Ponte del Formager, Dorsoduro 366 ■ 041 528 63 96
■ Closed Tue ■ €€

One of the city's top restaurants, specializing in game from the Veneto when in season. Extensive wine list.

7 Suzie Café
MAP B5 ■ Campo S Basilio, Dorsoduro 1527
■ €

This great bar, frequented by students, serves sandwiches, pasta and salads.

8 Pasticceria Tonolo
MAP K4 ■ Crosera S Pantalon, Dorsoduro 3764 ■ 041 523 72 09 ■ Closed Mon ■ €

One of the city's best pastry shops. Delicious, freshly baked almond biscuits and mini pizzas are recommended.

9 Gelateria Il Doge
MAP K5 ■ Campo S Margherita, Dorsoduro 3058A ■ 041 523 46 07
■ Closed Dec & Jan ■ €

Treat yourself to the *zuppa del doge* (candied fruit, egg custard and sponge cake soaked in Marsala) at this great ice-cream parlour.

Linea d'Ombra

10 Linea d'Ombra
MAP D5 ■ Ponte dell'Umiltà, Dorsoduro 19 ■ 041 241 18 81
■ Closed Tue, Dec–Feb ■ €€€

Enjoy the waterside setting behind the landmark Salute church. Specialities on the menu include tuna tartare and sea bass in a salt crust.

PRICE CATEGORIES

For a three-course meal for one with half a bottle of wine (or equivalent meal), taxes and extra charges.

€ under €40   €€ €40–60   €€€ over €60

See map on pp96–7

⟦TOP 10⟧ Cannaregio

Accounting for the huge crescent between the northern bank of the Grand Canal and the lagoon, the bustling *sestiere* of Cannaregio reaches from the railway station to the city hospital. It was home to Marco Polo and artists Titian and Tintoretto, and boasts landmark churches such as Madonna dell'Orto *(see p53)* along with the old Jewish Ghetto. Named after the *canne* (reeds) that once filled its marshes, it is crossed by Strada Nova, the city's main thoroughfare, but also contains Venice's narrowest alley, the 58-cm- (23-inch-) wide Calle Varisco. This vibrant area has its own market, craft workshops and rowing clubs, while relaxation comes at the string of shady parks and laid-back cafés and bars that line the maze of backstreet canals.

Campo dei Mori

AREA MAP OF CANNAREGIO

0 metres 300
0 yards 300

1 Ca' d'Oro

MAP N1 ▪ Calle Ca' d'Oro, Cannaregio 3932 ▪ 041 520 03 45 ▪ Open 8:15am–2pm Mon, 8:15am–7:15pm Tue–Sun ▪ Limited disabled access ▪ Admission charge ▪ www.cadoro.org

Behind the palace's beautiful Gothic tracery is a column-filled courtyard paved with coloured tesserae. Inside is the Galleria Franchetti, a collection of paintings, sculptures and ceramics donated to the State by Baron Giorgio Franchetti in 1916, along with the building. One highlight is Andrea Mantegna's *St Sebastian* (1560) pierced by arrows "like a hedgehog", in the portico leading to a loggia overlooking the Grand Canal. An ornate 15th-century staircase leads to 16th-century Flemish tapestries on the second floor *(see p50)*.

Jewish Ghetto, once a closed island

2 Jewish Ghetto

MAP C1 ▪ Museo Ebraico, Campo del Ghetto Nuovo, Cannaregio 2902/B ▪ 041 715 359 ▪ Open 10am–5:30pm Sun–Fri (to 7pm Jun–Sep) ▪ Closed public and Jewish holidays ▪ Admission charge

The word "ghetto" originated in Venice, derived from *getto* (casting) due to an old iron foundry here. As of 1492, many Jewish refugees reached Venice after expulsion from Spain and in 1527 they were obliged by law to move to this area. Subject to a curfew to prevent their fraternizing with local women, they slept behind locked gates, their island circled by an armed patrol boat. Waves of arrivals saw each language group build its own synagogue and raise the buildings to seven floors in height. Today around 30 Jews still live in the ghetto, while a further 470 reside in other parts of the city. The synagogues can be visited with a guide, and there's the Museo Ebraico (museum of sacred objects).

3 Corte Seconda del Milion

MAP Q2

The restructured Malibran Theatre, situated in this photogenic square, was erected in the 1790s on the site of a house, where the famous 13th-century explorer Marco Polo was born *(see p44)*. Other early Gothic buildings remain, their timber overhangs set off by bright-red geraniums. Along with the adjoining bridge, the square was named in honour of the explorer whose stories about the Orient in *Il Milione* continue to inspire travellers.

THE JEWS IN VENICE

Banned by Republic law from practising manual trades, many Jews were skilled doctors or moneylenders. Most were refugees from other parts of Europe, and they are credited with introducing rice-based dishes to Venetian cuisine. As remembered by a memorial in the ghetto, few returned from the Nazi camps of World War II.

④ Santa Maria dei Miracoli

MAP Q2 ▪ Campo dei Miracoli, Cannaregio ▪ 041 275 04 62 ▪ Open 10am–5pm Mon–Sat ▪ Admission charge ▪ www.chorusvenezia.org

A "jewellery box" of marble slabs and exquisite bas-reliefs, this Renaissance church was named after a miracle-working icon from 1409, said to have resuscitated a drowned man and now enshrined in the main altar *(see p52)*.

Santa Maria dei Miracoli

⑤ Campo dei Mori

MAP D1

In this odd, funnel-shaped square your attention is drawn to three statues of Arabian-style "Moors" – but neither North African nor Muslim, they hailed from Morea in Greece. Rioba, Sandi and Afani Mastelli were medieval traders who made their home in the family palace around the corner. Next to the bridge over Rio della Sensa is a doorway marked No. 3399, once the home of renowned 16th-century artist Tintoretto *(see p48)*.

⑥ Farmacia Ponci

MAP D2 ▪ Strada Nova, Cannaregio 2233/A

The "Casa degli Speziali", the oldest pharmacy in Venice, carries on its business in modern premises alongside its restored 16th-century rooms. Displayed on original briarwood shelving adorned with Baroque statues in Arolla pinewood are rows of 17th-century porcelain jars used for storing medicinal ingredients; for safety reasons, poisons were kept in a rear room. Pharmacies in Venice were strictly regulated and numbered 518 in 1564, the year their guild was formed.

⑦ Fondamente della Misericordia and degli Ormesini

MAP C2

Parallel to the Strada Nova but worlds away from the tourist bustle, these adjoining quaysides have a real neighbourhood feel. There's a good sprinkling of *osterie* (wine bars) alongside Mexican and Middle Eastern restaurants, a continuation of former trade links: the word *"ormesini"* derives from a rich fabric traded through Hormuz, now in Iran, and imitated in Florence and Venice. Ormesini leads into Misericordia and to the towering red-brick Scuola Grande building. Used as the city's basketball team headquarters for many years, it occasionally opens for temporary exhibitions.

Fondamente della Misericordia

8 Palazzo Labia

MAP C2 ■ Campo S Geremia,
Cannaregio ■ Closed to the public

Abandoned when its wealthy merchant owners fled to Vienna at the
fall of the Republic, this 17th-century
palace overlooking the Canal di
Cannaregio acted as a silk factory,
saw-mill and primary school, but
was badly damaged in 1945 when a
boat loaded with munitions blew up
in front of it. Luckily, the wonderful
ballroom frescoed by Tiepolo has
been restored. The palace belongs to
RAI, the state broadcasting service.

9 Chiesa di San Giobbe

MAP B2 ■ Campo S Giobbe,
Cannaregio ■ Open 10am–1:30pm
Mon–Sat ■ Admission charge
■ www.chorusvenezia.org

This church is a bit of a hotch-potch
after undergoing numerous modifi-
cations before it was suppressed
under Napoleon. An oratory and a
paupers' hospital, it was founded in
the 14th-century, with funding from
Doge Cristoforo Moro
and decorations by
Pietro Lombardo.
Altarpieces by
Giovanni Bellini and
Vittorio Carpaccio
now hang in the
Accademia
Galleries (see pp30–
31), but still here
are a 1445 triptych
by Vivarini in the
sacristy and a lovely
Nativity (1540) by Girolamo Savoldo.

Nativity by
Savoldo

10 Fondamente Nuove

MAP E2

This lagoon-side pavement, opposite
the cemetery island of San Michele
(see p118), is an important jumping-
off point for ferries to the northern
islands and sports one of the city's
rare petrol stations. The ample
quaysides were not constructed and
paved until the mid-1500s; until then
the waterfront reached back to
Titian's garden (No. 5113, Calle
Larga dei Botteri), giving unobstruc-
ted views of the Alps on a clear day.

▶ **MORNING**

Begin the day with the Galleria
Franchetti in the lovely Ca d'Oro
(see p103), but leave plenty of
time for the balconies that overlook the Grand Canal and
the mosaics in the courtyard.
Afterwards, follow **Strada Nova** in
the direction of the railway station
to the **Bottega del Caffè** (Calle del
Pistor, Cannaregio 1903 • 041 714
232 • Closed Wed) for the best coffee in Cannaregio. Only minutes
away is the fascinating **Jewish
Ghetto** (see p103), where you can
take an informative guided tour
of the many remaining
synagogues in the area.

🍴 For a revitalizing break, lunch
at **Hostaria alla Fontana** is
recommended (Fondamenta di
Cannaregio, Cannaregio 1102 • 041
715 077 • Closed Apr–Oct: Tue;
Nov–Mar: Sun).

AFTERNOON

Wander up the canal towards
Ponte dei Tre Archi (see p56) and
the **Chiesa di San Giobbe** (closes
at 1:30pm). Return over the bridge
and head for **Fondamenta della
Sacca**, which affords good views
of the Dolomites on a clear day.
Many ways lead east from here,
but try to take in the church of
Madonna dell'Orto (see p53) for
the Tintoretto paintings, then
Campo dei Mori to see the house
where the artist once lived.

On Fondamenta Ormesini, an
energetic young team awaits at **Al
Timon** with a glass of one of their
north Italian wines (Fondamenta
Ormesini, Cannaregio 2754 • 041
524 60 66 • Closed Wed).

See map on pp102–3 ←

Specialist Shops

(1) Tà Kalà

MAP D2 ▪ Strada Nova, Cannaregio 4391/C

Close to Campo SS Apostoli, this gift shop is a stockist of fascinating holograms, Murano glass delights, masks and chunky jewellery.

(2) Mori & Bozzi
MAP D2 ▪ Rio Terrà della Maddalena, Cannaregio 2367

One of the best shoe shops in Venice, offering an irresistible selection of women's footwear, clothes and accessories.

(3) San Leonardo Market
MAP C2 ▪ Rio Terrà San Leonardo ▪ Mon–Sat

In the morning and late afternoon this area functions as a lively open-air produce market. In autumn the air is thick with the aroma of roasting chestnuts.

San Leonardo Market

(4) Lili e Paolo Darin
MAP C2 ▪ Salizzada S Geremia, Cannaregio 317

Come here for original handmade glass beads in brilliant hues and myriad shapes, window hangings and Christmas decorations.

(5) Il Pirata
MAP Q2 ▪ Salizzada S Canciano, Cannaregio 5559

This shop organizes mask-making courses for both adults and children. You can also observe the craftsmen creating a mask from scratch.

Paintings for sale at Codex

(6) Codex
MAP C2 ▪ Fondamenta Ormesini, Cannaregio 2778

This studio and exhibition space of resident artists Nelson Kishi and Robin Frood sells original drawings, paintings, prints and posters.

(7) La Compagnia delle Perle
MAP P2 ▪ Calle Dolfin, Cannaregio 5622

This Aladdin's cave of a jewellery emporium has necklaces in any material from glass to horn or tin. Or you can buy beads to make your own.

(8) Salmoiraghi & Vigano
MAP D2 ▪ Strada Nova, Cannaregio 3928–3930

Italian spectacles are stylish and good value, and this well-reputed optometrist can make up prescription glasses the same day.

(9) Marco Polo Bookshop
MAP Q2 ▪ Calle del Teatro Malibran, Cannaregio 5886/A

This friendly, well-stocked store carries English-language volumes on Venice, as well as offering a book-exchange programme.

(10) Gianni Basso
MAP E2 ▪ Calle del Fumo, Cannaregio 5306

The marvellous handmade stationery on offer at this shop is made by a modest artisan and is popular with international VIPs.

Places to Eat

 Ristorante Al Fontego dei Pescatori

MAP D2 ■ Calle Priuli, Cannaregio 3726 ■ 041 520 05 38 ■ No disabled access ■ €

Classy seafood restaurant with a lovely courtyard for summer dining, noted for its seasonal specialities.

 Il Gelatone

MAP D2 ■ Rio Terrà della Maddalena, Cannaregio 2063 ■ 041 720 631 ■ €

Try the creamy and delicious *bacio* (kiss) of hazelnut and chocolate.

3 Brek

MAP B2 ■ Lista di Spagna, Cannaregio 124 ■ €

A self-service restaurant open from breakfast to dinner. Everything prepared as you wait.

4 Taverna del Campiello Remer

MAP D3 ■ Campiello Remer, Cannaregio 5701 ■ 041 522 87 89 ■ Closed Wed ■ No disabled access ■ €€€

This converted warehouse has upturned barrels as tables and offers a delicious buffet menu.

5 Il Santo Bevitore

MAP D2 ■ Campo S Fosca, Cannaregio 2393 ■ Closed Sun ■ €

Enjoy a drink and snack at this laid-back bar with live music.

6 Antica Mola

MAP C2 ■ Fondamenta degli Ormesini, Cannaregio 2800 ■ 041 717 492 ■ Closed Wed, Aug ■ €€

This is a friendly family trattoria with a garden and canal-side dining.

7 Al Parlamento

MAP B2 ■ Fondamenta Savorgnan, Cannaregio 511 ■ 041 244 02 14 ■ €

Appetizing, simple meals are served at this canal-side café where you can watch the boats go by.

Canal-side dining tables at Da Rioba

8 Da Rioba

MAP D2 ■ Fondamenta della Misericordia, Cannaregio 2553 ■ 041 524 43 79 ■ Closed Mon ■ €€–€€€

The impeccably presented Venetian fish-based dishes on the menu at this restaurant are given a tasteful modern twist.

9 Osteria Anice Stellato

MAP C1 ■ Fondamenta della Sensa, Cannaregio 3272 ■ 041 720 744 ■ Closed Mon & Tue, 2 weeks in Aug ■ €€

It is important to book well ahead for this popular place. Among the culinary delights on offer are fish and meat dishes, as well as a wonderful *zabaglione* dessert.

10 La Bottega Ai Promessi Sposi

MAP P1 ■ Calle dell'Oca, Cannaregio 4367 ■ 041 241 27 47 ■ Closed Mon & Wed lunch ■ €

This low-key restaurant offers diners tasty *cicheti* (bar snacks) while friendly staff serve more substantial traditional Venetian fare.

PRICE CATEGORIES

For a three-course meal for one with half a bottle of wine (or equivalent meal), taxes and extra charges.

....

€ under €40   €€ €40–60   €€€ over €60

See map on pp102–3

🔟 Castello

Named after a castle possibly built here in Roman times, Castello is the "fishtail" of Venice. The western half of the district is crammed with historic highlights such as the churches of SS Giovanni e Paolo and San Zaccaria *(see p52)*. However, half of Castello is taken up with shipbuilding, focusing on the historic Arsenale. The tree-lined Giardini is the venue for the Biennale *(see p111)*.

Riva degli Schiavoni

AREA MAP OF CASTELLO

1 Riva degli Schiavoni
MAP F4

Thronging with tour groups and packed with souvenir stalls, this quayside affords a lovely promenade past majestic palaces (now mostly hotels) and a much photographed 1887 monument to the first king of Italy, Vittorio Emanuele. It is linked to Piazza San Marco by the elegant Istrian stone bridge Ponte della Paglia, named after the *paglia* (straw) once unloaded from barges here. This is also the best place for taking pictures of the Bridge of Sighs. At the eastern end is the Ca' di Dio ("house of God"), a 13th-century hospice for pilgrims en route to the Holy Land.

2 Hotel Danieli
An enchanting 15th-century palace with a pink Gothic façade set on the magnificent waterfront near Piazza San Marco. After a string of aristocratic proprietors, it was taken over in 1822 by Joseph da Niel, who turned it into a hotel with an illustrious guest list, including Dickens, Wagner and Ruskin. In the 1940s an annexe was added amid great controversy – since 1102 no dwelling over one floor had been allowed on the site. The redeeming feature of the 1940s wing is the roof restaurant *(see p146)*.

Eye-catching front of Hotel Danieli

3 Santa Maria della Pietà
MAP F4 ▪ Riva degli Schiavoni, Castello 3700 ▪ Open 10:15am–noon & 3–5pm Tue–Fri; 10:15am–1pm & 2–5pm Sat & Sun ▪ Admission charge ▪ www.pietavenezia.org

Inextricably linked with the composer and musician Antonio Vivaldi, this Classical-fronted church belonged to the adjoining home for foundlings where he taught. Come to an evening concert to appreciate Tiepolo's uplifting ceiling fresco, exalting music and the young choristers, identifiable by the sprigs of pomegranate blossom they wear. The choir stalls accommodated both the singers and the nobility, who were not expected to mix with the commoners.

Santa Maria della Pietà

4 Arsenale
MAP G3 ▪ **Castello**

Aptly named after the Arab word *darsina'a* ("house of industry"), Venice's formidable Arsenale shipyards at their peak employed an army of 16,000 to produce the fleets that sailed the Mediterranean, spreading and protecting the influence of the Republic through trade deals and naval superiority. With its innovative assembly-line system, the Arsenale could construct a galley in a few hours, notably in 1574 while the French king Henry III enjoyed a banquet. The stone lions that guard the entrance hail from Greek islands looted by Venetian commanders.

Crenellated entrance to Arsenale

5 San Pietro di Castello
MAP H4 ▪ **Chiesa di San Pietro di Castello** ▪ **Open 10am–5pm Mon–Sat** ▪ **Admission charge** ▪ **www.chorusvenezia.org**

It is hard to imagine that Venice's religious headquarters were here until 1807, when the Basilica San Marco became the city's cathedral. Linked to the rest of Castello by two broad bridges, San Pietro attracts artists for its evocative, forlorn air, and fun-lovers for the late-June neighbourhood fair. Art lovers come for the church with work by Veronese and Coducci.

6 Campo Santi Giovanni e Paolo
MAP E3

Dominated by the brick façade of the Gothic church SS Giovanni e Paolo, this breezy square welcomes visitors with a flotilla of outdoor cafés. Worthy of contemplation is one of the world's most magnificent equestrian statues, a stylized 15th-century portrait of the great *condottiere* Bartolomeo Colleoni. He left a legacy to the city on the condition that his statue be erected in front of San Marco, craftily "interpreted" by the governors as the nearby Scuola Grande di San Marco. Gracefully decorated with arches and trompe l'oeil panels by Lombard masters, the former confraternity serves as the public hospital.

7 Campo Santa Maria Formosa
MAP E3 ▪ **Chiesa di Santa Maria Formosa** ▪ **Open 10am–5pm Mon–Sat** ▪ **Admission charge** ▪ **www.chorusvenezia.org**

A lovely rounded church on this sun-blessed square appears to spread in all directions, the result of a 7th-century bishop's vision of the *formosa* ("shapely") Virgin Mary's request that it be built where "a white cloud came to rest". Artworks are by Vivarini and Palma il Vecchio. The square is a good place for a picnic or a game of football, in lieu of the bullfights and re-enactments of Venice's conquests held here in the olden days.

8 Chiesa di San Francesco della Vigna
MAP F3 ▪ **Campo S Francesco della Vigna, Castello 2786** ▪ **041 520 61 02** ▪ **Open 8am–12:30pm, 3–7pm Mon–Sat, 3–6:30pm Sun**

In the back alleys of Castello, this Franciscan church sports a combination of architectural styles courtesy of both Sansovino and Palladio *(see p49)*, who designed the façade. The colonnaded cloister can be seen while you're admiring Giovanni Bellini's *Madonna and Child* (1507). Another highlight is Veronese's *Virgin and Child with Saints* (1551). Playgrounds have replaced the 13th-century *vigna* (vineyards).

Campo Santi Giovanni e Paolo

9 Via Garibaldi and Giardini

MAP H5

A pleasant avenue lined with cafés and a market, Via Garibaldi was named when the eponymous general marched into Venice in 1866 as part of his campaign for Unification. Take a stroll to the Giardini (public gardens). To make way for the park in 1807, architect Selva (see p49) demolished four churches and convents and a sailors' hospice.

Via Garibaldi

10 Ospedaletto

MAP F3 ▪ Barbaria delle Tole, Castello 6691 ▪ Open 2:30–6:30pm Thu–Sat (Nov–Mar: 3–6pm)

The sculptures on the façade of this almshouse church, built in 1575, were added by Longhena in 1674. Pass through the church to the Sala della Musica, where female wards of the orphanage once gave concerts.

THE VENICE BIENNALE

The Giardini and its beautiful tree-lined avenues (**below**) were inaugurated as an international exhibition area in 1895 under the entrepreneur Count Volpi di Misurata. Every two years, more than 50 countries send artists to represent them, each with their own pavilion custom-designed by some of the world's leading architects, such as Alvar Aalto, Carlo Scarpa and James Stirling.

A DAY IN CASTELLO

▶ **MORNING**

After a visit to the Gothic church on **Campo Santi Giovanni e Paolo**, wander through the city's **hospital**. Although it is now ultra-modern inside, you can still appreciate the wonderful Renaissance façade, and a series of ancient courtyards and confraternity buildings. Continue the historic theme with a coffee and cake at old-style Rosa Salva (Campo SS Giovanni e Paolo, Castello 6779 • 041 522 79 49).

Take a stroll, via **Campo Santa Maria Formosa**, to **Campo San Zaccaria** and the church with its Bellini painting, and **Scuola di San Giorgio degli Schiavoni** (see pp54–5) for its Carpaccio works. For lunch, **Via Garibaldi** is a good bet, at one of the cafés or at Sottoprova (041 520 64 93 • Closed Mon).

AFTERNOON

Head east along **Via Garibaldi**, and detour briefly into the shady avenue for the statue of Giuseppe Garibaldi and his followers. After a visit to the island of **San Pietro di Castello**, make your way back via the lagoon and the **Giardini**. A poignant sculpture to the female partisans of World War II can be seen at water level.

Head in the direction of San Marco, just past the mouth of Via Garibaldi. On the embankment is **Angiò Bar**, the perfect spot for a Venetian sunset together with a glass of wine, not to mention all manner of delicious snacks (Riva di S Biasio, Castello 2142 • 041 277 85 55 • Closed Tue).

See map on pp108–9

Specialist Shops

1 Le Ceramiche
MAP F4 ▪ Calle del Pestrin, Castello 3876

In a tiny atelier close to the Arsenale (see p110), Alessandro Merlin creates original platters, cups and tiles, with black and white designs based on lagoon fish or human figures.

2 Pastificio Le Spighe
MAP G4 ▪ Via Garibaldi, Castello 1341

Although it seems a normal grocery store at first sight, behind the façade this hive of industry produces a marvellous range of home-made pasta and stocks gourmet olive oils and olive paste.

3 Papier Mâché
MAP R3 ▪ Calle Lunga Santa Maria Formosa, Castello 5175

One of the few authentic mask shops in town. It also sells beautiful ceramics.

4 Il Papiro
MAP E4 ▪ Calle delle Bande, Castello 5275

Tempting gifts in the shape of marbled paper-covered boxes, greeting cards and writing paper with artistic letterheads.

5 Bragorà
MAP F4 ▪ Salita Sant'Antonin, Castello 3496

Eclectic mix of design, art and creative objects, many of them sourced from local designers.

Books stacked at Libreria Acqua Alta

6 Libreria Acqua Alta
MAP R3 ▪ Calle Longa S Maria Formosa, Castello 5176

A fascinating bookshop with ancient volumes piled high inside a gondola and plenty of Venetian-specific literature.

Venetian mask

7 Miotto
MAP R4 ▪ Salizzada Zorzi, Castello 4945

Artistic homewares – from Moorish lampstands to candelabra and ornate mirrors – are to be found amid the cornucopia of delights at this shop.

8 Ratti
MAP F4 ▪ Salizzada S Lio, Castello 5825

This eclectic shop sells household items such as the quintessential Italian coffee pot, along with mobile phones and hardware.

9 Corte delle Fate
MAP E3 ▪ Salizzada S Lio, Castello 5690

Ultra-modern footwear and quirky accessories are available here in the shape of bags, jewellery and garments for the young.

10 Giovanna Zanella
MAP Q3 ▪ Calle Carminati, Castello 5641

A must for all serious shoppers – quirky handmade shoes in a fabulous range of incredible designs.

Stylish Bragorà

Places to Eat

1 Taverna Olandese Volante

MAP E3 ■ Campo S Lio, Castello 5658 ■ Closed Sun lunch ■ €

Lively bar serving draught beer and where the rolls are named after pirates and the salads after ships – try the "Galeone" with prawn and hard-boiled egg.

2 Pasticceria Ponte delle Paste

MAP Q3 ■ Ponte del Pistor, Castello 5991 ■ 041 522 28 89 ■ No disabled access ■ €

Luscious cream cakes and fragrant buttery pastries can be enjoyed here with coffee or tea.

3 Boutique del Gelato

MAP E3 ■ Salizzada S Lio, Castello 5727 ■ 041 522 32 83 ■ Closed Dec & Jan ■ €

There's inevitably a queue outside this popular *gelateria*. Try the tangy *limone* (lemon) or *fragola* (strawberry) ice cream or creamy *gianduiotto* (hazelnut-chocolate).

4 Trattoria dai Tosi Piccoli

MAP H5 ■ Secco Marina, Castello 736–738 ■ 041 523 71 02 ■ Closed Wed & Christmas ■ €

This cheery restaurant is especially popular when the Biennale art show (see p72) is held. Mouthwatering *pasta della casa* (house pasta) includes seafood and vegetables.

5 Trattoria Giorgione

MAP G4 ■ Via Guiseppe Garibaldi, Castello 1533 ■ 041 522 87 27 ■ Closed Wed ■ €

After serving his fish specialities, owner Lucio entertains guests with Venetian folk songs.

6 Alla Rivetta

MAP E4 ■ Ponte S Provolo, Castello 4625 ■ 041 528 73 02 ■ Closed Mon ■ €€

Friendly eatery with a wonderful seafood window display.

7 Alla Mascareta

MAP E3 ■ Calle Lunga S Maria Formosa, Castello 5183 ■ 338 893 91 22 ■ Closed Sun lunch, 4 weeks Dec–Jan ■ €

Upmarket bar for wine lovers. Also serves antipasti and main dishes.

Alla Mascareta

8 Alle Testiere

MAP E3 ■ Calle del Mondo Nuovo, Castello 5801 ■ 041 522 72 20 ■ Closed Sun & Mon, Aug ■ €€€

This is a tiny and cosy restaurant that has an unusual selection of fish, cheese and wines.

9 Le Spighe

MAP G4 ■ Via Guiseppe Garibaldi, Castello 1341 ■ 041 523 81 73 ■ Closed Sun ■ €

Great vegan and vegetarian eatery and food emporium – an absolute must for those who don't eat meat.

10 Al Covo

MAP F4 ■ Campiello de la Pescaria, Castello 3968 ■ 041 522 38 12 ■ Closed Wed & Thu, 1 week Aug, 4 weeks Dec–Jan ■ €€€

Come here for sophisticated fish dishes and pair them with choices from the Italian wine list.

See map on pp108–9 ←

TOP10 The Northern Lagoon

The northern lagoon is dotted with mud flats and abandoned islands where rambling monasteries lie crumbling in the sun, backed by sweeping views of snow-capped mountains. Refugees from the mainland, fleeing the Huns, first settled on Torcello, which grew with the additional influx of influential religious orders. Today, however, only a handful of islands are still inhabited – glassmaking Murano is the most important, while Burano, Mazzorbo and Sant'Erasmo have skeletal populations of fishermen and market gardeners. Salt pans, such as Le Saline, were a source of employment until as late as 1913.

Glass birds on Murano

AREA MAP OF THE NORTHERN LAGOON

Murano

Canale degli Angeli

Venier ③

CPO SAN DONATO

Da Mula ②

Museo

Serenella ④ Murano ③

Navagero

FONDAMENTA VETRAI

CALLE BRESSAGIO

Faro

Colonna

0 metres 400
0 yards 400

Torcello ① ⑨
Torcello

Mazzorbo
Mazzorbo ④ Burano ② Burano
⑥ ⑦ ⑩ ⑤ ⑧ ⑧ ⑨ ⑩

San Francesco del Deserto ⑤

Punta Vela

Laguna Veneto

See Murano inset, above

Murano

Lazzaretto Nuovo
Lazzaretto ⑧
Nuovo
Capannone

Chiesa
Sant'Erasmo ⑦

Punta Sabbioni ⑩
Punta Sabbioni

Cimitero ⑥ San Michele

Fondamente Nove

Le Vignole

Vignole

VENICE

S. Pietro
Certosa ⑨ Certosa

0 kilometres 1
0 miles 1

Lido

① **Top 10 Sights**
see pp117–19

① **Places to Eat**
see p121

① **Specialist Shops**
see p120

Previous pages Cappella degli Scrovegni, Padua

1 Torcello
See pp36–7.

2 Burano
MAP H1 ■ Ferry No. 12 from Fondamente Nuove or S Zaccaria

A haven for artists, Burano takes pride in its brightly painted houses, fish and lace-making. The islanders cherish an old legend about a faithful sailor who resisted the Sirens' call and was rewarded with a magnificent veil of magical foam for his bride, later worked into lace, a trade that brought worldwide fame and fortune to the isolated fisherfolk. These days, old women still strain their eyes with patient stitches, but many articles are imported from abroad. The island's dramatically leaning bell tower is visible from afar.

3 Murano
MAP G2 ■ Vaporetto lines 4.1 & 4.2 from Fondamente Nuove & S Zaccaria, 3 from P Roma or seasonal lines

Long synonymous with glassmaking, Murano brought blowing and fusion techniques to extraordinary heights in the 1500s, and so closely guarded were the trade secrets that skilled craftsmen could migrate only under pain of death. Though Venice's glass monopoly lasted only until the 17th century, its fame lives on. A visit to the Glass Museum (Museo del Vetro) with its 4,000 exhibits is a must *(see p54)*. Don't be put off by the reps who invite tourists to see a furnace and showroom; it's a unique opportunity to watch the glassblowers at work and is free. However, if you accept a free boat trip from San Marco to a glass factory, you're expected to make your own way back by *vaporetto* if you don't buy anything. Glassmaking aside, Murano is a lovely place with canals, alleyways and friendly islanders.

4 Mazzorbo
MAP H1 ■ Ferry No. 12 from Fondamente Nuove

This pretty, verdant island exudes a tranquil air as locals tend their vineyards or artichoke fields.

Wicker cages for fattening up *moleche* (soft-shelled crabs) hang over the water and the produce can be sampled in the low-key trattorias. Amid the scattering of houses are bold modern council blocks, which are painted in pastel hues. Mazzorbo has its own boat stop but is also joined to Burano by a long timber footbridge.

Quaint waterfront of Mazzorbo

5 San Francesco del Deserto
MAP H1 ■ Taxi launch from Burano's landing stage ■ Monastery: open 9–11am, 3–5pm Tue–Sun ■ Donation ■ www.sanfrancescodeldeserto.it

A short distance from Burano, this attractive island of cypress trees is home to a Franciscan monastery. According to legend it was founded by St Francis in person, on his way back from preaching missions in Egypt and Palestine in 1220. In May, clad in their brown habits and sandals, the monks attend the Vogalonga regatta in their heavy-duty boat, much to the delight of the Venetian crowds *(see p72)*.

San Francesco del Deserto

San Michele cemetery

6 San Michele

MAP G2 ▪ Ferry Nos. 4.1 & 4.2 from Fondamente Nove & S Zaccaria ▪ Cemetery: open 7:30am–6pm daily (closes 4pm Oct–Mar)

San Michele became the city cemetery in 1826, in the wake of a Napoleonic decree that the dead should be buried far from city dwellings to improve hygiene standards. Entry to the cemetery is via a lovely Gothic portal surmounted by St Michael at odds with a dragon, and through the monk's colonnaded cloister. But don't neglect to visit the pretty marble-façaded church next door, designed by Mauro Coducci in 1469 (see p49). On All Souls' Day (2 November), the place is crowded with relatives paying a visit to their dear departed. However, unless you're a famous resident like Ezra Pound, Igor Stravinsky or Sergei Diaghilev, your bones are dug up after 10 years and placed in an urn to make room for someone else.

7 Sant'Erasmo

MAP H2 ▪ Ferry No. 13 from Fondamente Nuove

Just over 4 km (2.5 miles) long and 1 km (0.5 miles) at the broadest point, Sant'Erasmo offers tranquil countryside, praised enthusiastically by the Romans who built sumptuous villas here. A couple of rickety old motorcars occasionally bump along the lanes, but bicycles and boats are still the main form of transport. The main activity here is market gardening, particularly the production of delicious asparagus and artichokes, which prosper on the sandy soil and are a mainstay of Rialto Market (see p34). There is also a small stretch of sandy beach.

Asparagus and artichokes

8 Lazzaretto Nuovo

MAP H2 ▪ Ferry No. 13 from Fondamente Nuove ▪ Tours Apr–Oct: 9:45am & 4:30pm Sat & Sun ▪ www.lazzarettonuovo.com

Up until the 1700s this island, across the water from Sant'Erasmo, served as a quarantine station for merchant ships entering the lagoon and suspected of carrying the plague. Together with Sant'Erasmo it held up to 10,000 people during the 1576 pestilence, while cargoes were fumigated with rosemary and juniper in temporary shelters. Later converted into a military stronghold,

---

LAGOON FLORA AND FAUNA

The lagoon abounds in gilt-head bream, sea bass, clams, cuttlefish and crabs, all prey for wetland waterfowl such as swans, egrets (**below**), cormorants and the rare black-winged stilts. Sea lavender blooms on land masses, rock samphire clings to crumbling masonry, while glasswort thrives in the salt-ridden marshes.

it now swarms with archaeology enthusiasts, intent on unearthing its secrets, and Italian students attending summer camps.

9 Certosa
MAP H2

Inhabited by religious communities for more than 600 years, the "charterhouse" island went the way of many of its neighbours under occupation by French, Austrian and Italian forces, though currently as the property of the City Council it is slowly being cleaned up as a public park. It can be visited in summer months, though opening times vary; Alilaguna Blu boats *(see p139)* stop here seasonally. From the Lido–Punta Sabbioni ferry the impressive ramparts of Sanmicheli's 16th-century Forte di Sant'Andrea can be seen, much as they must have appeared in the past to any hostile vessels that dared to enter the lagoon unbidden.

10 Punta Sabbioni
Ferry No. 14 from Lido & S Zaccaria

This locality clings to the promontory extending westward from the mainland – a continuous string of beach resorts equipped with spacious campsites. Alongside sleepy backwaters and canals is Punta Sabbioni ("big sandy point"), a busy bus-ferry terminal that bustles with summer holiday-makers. It came into being as sand accumulated behind the 1,100-m (3,600-ft) breakwater erected to protect the port mouth and littoral. The stretch offers lovely seaside strolls.

Punta Sabbioni

SAILING THE LAGOON

▶ MORNING

To save money, buy a one-day travel card and then take a *vaporetto* to **Murano** *(see p117)* to watch a glassmaking demonstration at a furnace or one of the workshops. Don't miss Murano's very own **Grand Canal**, before returning via Fondamenta Manin with its medieval porticoes for the turn-off towards the **Faro** (lighthouse) landing stage. Bar al Faro is a perfect place for coffee *(Fondamenta Piave 20, Murano • 041 739 724 • Closed Sun)*.

Take a ferry to **Burano** *(see p117)*. Either picnic on the famous Burano biscuits or lunch at Da Romano *(Piazza Galuppi 221, Burano • 041 730 030 • Closed Tue & Sun dinner, mid-Dec–early Feb)*, a popular meeting place for artists.

AFTERNOON

Pop over to **Torcello** *(see pp36–7)* by ferry for the awe-inspiring Byzantine mosaics in the basilica. Climb the bell tower for views of the lagoon and the Dolomite mountains, if weather conditions and visibility are favourable.

Take the ferry back to Burano and then head east, past low-lying islands and tidal flats towards Treporti. A stretch parallel to the sandy littoral separating the lagoon from the Adriatic Sea takes you to **Punta Sabbioni**, where a stopover is feasible for a drink on the jetty.

End the day sailing across the broad lagoon mouth, via the **Lido** *(see p123)*, back to **Piazza San Marco** *(see pp20–23)*.

See map on p116 ←

Specialist Shops

1 Cesare Sent
MAP G2 ■
Fondamenta Vetrai 8B, Murano

This talented artist, from a long line of glassmakers, transforms the ancient art of murrhine glassware into striking modern objects of beauty.

Cesare Sent glasswork

2 ArtStudio
MAP G2 ■

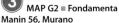

Fondamenta Rivalonga 48, Murano
Watch glass artist Davide Penso at work producing marvellous African-inspired glass beads.

3 Manin 56
MAP G2 ■ Fondamenta Manin 56, Murano

Striking etched bowls and slender wine glasses from Salviati flank international designer items in this wonderful collection.

4 Nason & Moretti
MAP G2 ■ Calle Dietro Gli Orti 12, Murano

This shop stocks a stunning collection of glassware created by these acclaimed Murano designers in a dazzling array of colours and styles. Well worth visiting.

5 Barovier & Toso
MAP G2 ■ Fondamenta Vetrai 28, Murano

The world's oldest family of glassmakers, the Baroviers are able to trace their ancestry back to the 13th century. They still produce stunning contemporary pieces.

6 Mazzega
MAP G2 ■ Fondamenta da Mula 147, Murano

Vast showrooms here display traditional and semi-modern glass designs, with an emphasis on chandeliers and vases.

7 CAM
MAP G2 ■ Piazzale Colonna 1, Murano

This is the first shop you see as you disembark at the Murano Colonna stop. It is an internationally known firm specializing in distinctive high-quality, modern pieces.

8 Pastificio e Panificio Giorgio Garbo
MAP H1 ■ Via S Mauro 336, Burano

Sample Burano's trademark vanilla-flavoured shortbread, *bussolai*, freshly baked in traditional rounds or "S" shapes.

9 Emilia Burano
MAP H1 ■ Via Galuppi 205, Burano

Superb laceware along with exquisite in-house designed linen collections at this family-run boutique.

10 Lidia Merletti d'Arte
MAP H1 ■ Via Galuppi 215, Burano

While the front of the shop is an emporium of lace tablecloths, hand towels and mats, the rear is a gallery with a priceless 18th-century wedding gown, a lace fan owned by Louis XIV and lace altarpieces.

Lidia Merletti d'Arte

Places to Eat

PRICE CATEGORIES

For a three-course meal for one with half a bottle of wine (or equivalent meal), taxes and extra charges.

€ under €40 €€ €40–60 €€€ over €60

1 Trattoria Busa alla Torre, Da Lele

MAP G2 ■ Campo S Stefano 3, Murano ■ 041 739 662 ■ Open for lunch year-round ■ No disabled access ■ €

Dine inside under timber rafters or out in the square. Start with ravioli filled with fish, but leave room for the nougat pastries.

2 Panificio Giovanni Marcato

MAP G2 ■ Fondamenta Rivalonga 16, Murano ■ 041 739 176 ■ Closed Sun ■ €

Delicious slices of pizza with tomato and olives, and traditional *zaletti* biscuits or luscious *pincetto*, sponge cake with chocolate.

3 Osteria La Perla Ai Bisatei

MAP G2 ■ Campo S Bernardo 6, Murano ■ 041 739 528 ■ Open for lunch only ■ No credit cards ■ No disabled access ■ €

Home-style cooking at good prices. The *fritto misto* seafood is superb.

4 Trattoria Valmarana

MAP G2 ■ Fondamenta Navagero 31, Murano ■ 041 739 313 ■ Open for lunch only ■ €

Stylish eating on a waterside terrace. Try *rombo al forno con patate e olive* (flounder with potatoes and olives).

5 Riva Rosa Ristorante

MAP H1 ■ Via S Maruo 296, Burano ■ 041 730 850 ■ Open for lunch and dinner (booking essential); closed Wed ■ €€€

Romantic roof and canal-side dining. Try the Rossini *aperitivo* with freshly juiced strawberries and prosecco.

6 Trattoria ai Cacciatori

MAP H1 ■ Fondamenta S Caterina 24, Mazzorbo ■ 041 730 118 ■ Closed Mon, 7 Jan–7 Feb ■ €

Cheaper than Burano, here you can savour potato dumplings with crab and, in autumn, local game.

Antica Trattoria alla Maddalena

7 Antica Trattoria alla Maddalena

MAP H1 ■ Fondamenta S Caterina 7B, Mazzorbo ■ 041 730 151 ■ Open for lunch and early dinner only; closed Thu, Jan ■ €

Try the spring artichokes or the roast duck with a light, local white wine.

8 Al Gatto Nero

MAP H1 ■ Fondamenta Giudecca 88, Burano ■ 041 730 120 ■ Closed Mon, 1st week Jul, 2 weeks in Nov ■ No disabled access ■ €€

Wonderful al fresco fish restaurant, surrounded by colourful houses.

9 Locanda Cipriani

MAP H1 ■ Piazza S Fosca 29, Torcello ■ 041 730 150 ■ Closed Nov–Dec: Mon & Tue; Jan–Feb ■ No disabled access ■ €€€

The house speciality is *filetto di San Pietro Carlina* (baked John Dory with tomato and capers).

10 Venissa

MAP H1 ■ Fondamenta S Caterina 3, Mazzorbo ■ 041 527 22 81 ■ Closed Tue (restaurant), Wed (osteria); Nov–Apr ■ €–€€€

Choose between low-key *osteria* and sophisticated restaurant serving locally grown produce.

See map on pp116

🔟 The Southern Lagoon and Venice Lido

The southern lagoon enjoys protection from the Adriatic Sea with shifting sand spits long transformed into a permanent littoral, the residential Lido, with the help of nature and man. The latter's efforts date back to the 6th century, but the earth and wicker barriers have since been modified into sturdy seawalls and massive parallel breakwaters at the shipping entrances of San Nicolò, Alberoni and Chioggia. On the lagoon's southwestern edge are fish farms and wild shallows where hunters and fishermen still roam, well clear of the Valle Averto

Chiesa del Santissimo Redentore, Giudecca

reserve run by the World Wildlife Fund for Nature (WWF). Closer to Venice itself is a cluster of sizeable islands such as majestic San Giorgio and populous Giudecca, then diminutive land masses such as Lazzaretto Vecchio, where plague victims were once quarantined but which has now been re-adapted as a home for stray dogs, a sanatorium acquired for private development as an exclusive resort, and countless other evocative abandoned places.

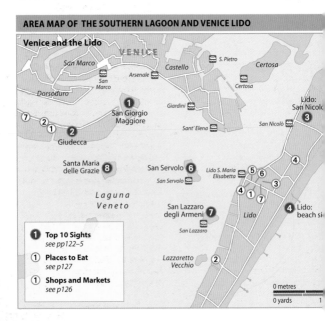

AREA MAP OF THE SOUTHERN LAGOON AND VENICE LIDO

Venice and the Lido

VENICE

San Marco
Castello
S. Pietro
Certosa
Arsenale
San Marco
Certosa
Dorsoduro
Lido: San Nicolò
Giardini
San Giorgio Maggiore ❶
San Nicolò ❸
❼ ❷ ❶ ❷
Sant' Elena
Giudecca
❹
Santa Maria delle Grazie ❽
San Servolo ❻
Lido S. Maria Elisabetta
❺ ❻
San Servolo
❹ ❶ ❼
❸
Laguna Veneto
San Lazzaro degli Armeni ❼
Lido
❹ Lido: beach side
San Lazzaro

❶ **Top 10 Sights**
see pp122–5

① **Places to Eat**
see p127

① **Shops and Markets**
see p126

Lazzaretto Vecchio ❷

0 metres
0 yards   1

Church of San Giorgio Maggiore

1 San Giorgio Maggiore

Fondazione Giorgio Cini (vaporetto No. 2) ■ **Open 10am–5pm (to 4pm Oct–Apr) Sat & Sun for guided visits (041 220 12 15)** ■ **Admission charge**

The island of cypresses is separated from the main body of Venice by St Mark's Basin and retains a quiet, meditative air. An ancient vineyard and salt pans were replaced by a landmark church by Andrea Palladio *(see p49)*, adjoining an elegant Benedictine monastery. It is now a scientific and cultural foundation and conference centre. At the rear is the open-air Teatro Verde, which is used for performances of contemporary dance and music.

2 Giudecca

Vaporetto Nos. 2, 4.1, 4.2

An S-shaped slice of land facing the sun-blessed Zattere, this residential garden island was first known as "Spina longa" for its fishbone form. It was renamed either after an early Jewish community or the *giudicati* (radical aristocrats) exiled here. Italian Renaissance artist Michelangelo spent three peaceful years here in voluntary exile from 1529. Much later it became an important industrial zone with shipbuilding and the immense Molino Stucky flour mill. Usually quiet and neighbourly, it comes to life with a vengeance for the mid-July Redentore festivities *(see p72)*.

3 Lido: San Nicolò

Jewish Cemetery: Bus A from S Maria Elisabetta or car ferry from Tronchetto ■ **Guided visits to the cemetery Mar–Sep (book ahead 041 715 359)** ■ **www.museoebraico.it**

The northern end of the Lido littoral, a key point in the Republic's defence, used to be equipped with impressive naval fortifications, and chains would be laid across the lagoon mouth as a deterrent to invaders. The historic Festa della Sensa celebration *(see p73)* is held offshore from the church of San Nicolò, founded in 1044 and a former Benedictine monastery, now a study centre. One visitable site is the 1386 Jewish cemetery. Alternatively, take a 35-minute mini cruise on the car ferry between Tronchetto car park and San Nicolò. Its high decks offer great views.

e Southern Lagoon

Venice
Lido
Area shown on map, left

...sina

Laguna
Veneto

③ ⑤ Malamocco

Alberoni

Golfo di Venezia

⑤ ⑨ San Pietro in Volta
⑥

⑨ Pellestrina

⑧ ⑨ ⑩
⑧ ⑨ ⑩
⑩ Chioggia

0 km   3
0 miles 3

San Nicolò, Lido

HEYDAY OF THE LIDO

Evidence of the Lido's "golden age" as Europe's leading seaside resort at the turn of the 20th century can still be seen in the magnificent Art Deco villas. Exemplary survivors are the Hotel des Bains and the Excelsior, built in 1907 as the world's largest hotel, complete with mock minarets. Before that, the Lido was appreciated for its healthy air.

4 Lido: Beach Side
Ferry Nos. 1, 5.1, 5.2, 6, 14

Manicured sand, raked daily, and neat rows of multicoloured bathing cabins and beach umbrellas sum up the Lido from June to September, made famous in Thomas Mann's novel *Death in Venice (see p46)*. Venetians spend their summers socializing in style here. Things liven up considerably for the 10-day International Film Festival in September *(see p62)*, when the shady streets are filled with film buffs and critics on bicycles.

5 Lido: Malamocco
Bus No. 11 or line B from S Maria Elisabetta

About midway along the Lido is the pretty, quiet village of Malamocco and it's now hard to imagine that it was the most important lagoon settlement soon after Roman times and the main port for Padua.

San Lazzaro degli Armeni

A storm and giant waves washed away the entire town in 1106, but it was later rebuilt in the vicinity on a smaller scale. It is appreciated for its 15th-century buildings, peaceful nature and rustic trattorias.

6 San Servolo
Ferry No. 20 from San Zaccaria
■ Guided visits 11:30am, 2:45pm **(book ahead 041 524 01 19)**

In 1648, 200 nuns exiled from Candia, Crete, by the Turks were lodged on this island, but after their numbers dwindled in 1725

it was given over to a sanatorium for psychiatric cases, although exclusively those of "comfortable circumstances". The roomy buildings are now shared by an international university and a trade school for artisans from all over Europe interested in restoration of stone and stucco techniques.

Student painting at San Servolo

7 San Lazzaro degli Armeni
Ferry line No. 20 from San Zaccaria
■ Open 3:20–5pm daily
■ Admission charge

Venice made a gift of this erstwhile leper colony to the Armenian monk, the Venerable Mechtar, forced out of the Peloponnese during one of his country's diasporas. Intent on fostering the Armenian culture and language, he founded a religious community here and set up a printing press that ran until 1994. Multilingual monks instruct visitors in Armenian history and lead tours through a small museum and a library of more than 100,000 volumes and precious illuminated manuscripts.

8 Santa Maria delle Grazie
Close to San Giorgio, this abandoned island used to be a hospice for pilgrims and was named after a miraculous image of the Virgin brought back from Constantinople and attributed to St Luke. Its colourful history features a series of religious orders and

churches, devastating fires, allotments, luxuriant gardens and the city's infectious diseases hospital. It is now private property with no public access.

⑨ San Pietro in Volta and Pellestrina

Bus-ferry No. 11 from the Lido or from Chioggia

This narrow 11-km (6.5-mile) central strip of land, linked to the Lido and Chioggia by ferry, is dotted with picturesque sleepy fishing communities, once famous for lacemaking and now renowned for champion rowers and a shipyard. The Genoese wiped out the villages during the 14th century, an event almost repeated during the disastrous 1966 floods – powerful waves broke over the seawall, forcing full-scale evacuation. The massive defensive barriers with their 14-m (46-ft) broad base were first erected in the 1700s, but have consequently needed large-scale reinforcement.

⑩ Chioggia

Ferry from Pellestrina or bus from Piazzale Roma

A lively fishing town, with elegant bridges over navigable canals. The friendly inhabitants have a reputation for lawlessness and bickering, and speak a distinctive dialect with a singsong inflection. Chioggia has a rich history, but its greatest moment came as the arena for the decisive battle in the 1378–9 war, when the Genoese came close to conquering Venice. In flat-bottomed boats the crafty locals lured the enemy into the lagoon, thus gaining the upper hand.

Cleaning fishing nets in Chioggia

A DAY ON THE LAGOON

> **MORNING**

From the Santa Maria Elisabetta ferry stop, either hire a bicycle or take bus B southwest along the lagoon edge for **Malamocco**. Wander through the peaceful village and over its bridge to the sea to take in the Adriatic and the impressive seawall. Then proceed with buses B or 11 through **Alberoni** and past the golf course for the vehicle ferry across the lagoon entrance. Get off at the second stop for **San Pietro in Volta**. Climb the high seawall for panoramic views of the sea, before turning lagoon-wards for the picturesque pastel-painted fishing settlement that spreads along the waterfront.

Have lunch at one of the trattorias (see p127) or a sandwich and glass of wine at one of the modest waterfront bars.

AFTERNOON

Further south the bus terminates at **Pellestrina**, a brightly painted fishing village flanked by an active shipyard. The passenger ferry to **Chioggia** is a beautiful half-hour cruise past mussel grounds punctuated with fisher huts perched on poles, via the Ca' Roman landing stage, which provides access to a beach. Chioggia is a lovely town to explore, with its traffic-free piazza lined with old palazzos and countless fish restaurants.

Indulge in a pre-dinner drink and some cicheti (bar snacks) at one of the laid-back cafés in the elegant Corso del Popolo.

See map on pp122–3

Shops and Markets

Rizzo delicatessen

① Rizzo
MAP H2 ■ **Gran Viale Santa Maria Elisabetta 16/20, Lido**

Unbeatable gourmet food from all over Italy – buffalo mozzarella, creamy Asiago cheese, cured Parma ham and gleaming olives. Pizza and focaccia can be found at the bread counter.

② General Market
MAP H2 ■ **Via Falier, Lido** ■ **Tue am**

Open-sided vans sell fresh produce, alongside designer-quality clothes, shoes and bags at approachable prices. Even if you don't buy anything, the lagoon setting looking over to the Venice skyline makes a trip worthwhile.

③ Erbalido
MAP H2 ■ **Via Negroponte 4/C, Lido**

Here you will find a traditional herbalist who can advise on natural remedies for minor ailments.

④ Arbor Boutique
MAP H2 ■ **Gran Viale Santa Maria Elisabetta 10, Lido**

The upmarket range of menswear and womenswear for sale at this clothes shop attracts both foreign and Italian customers.

⑤ Bruno Lazzari
MAP H2 ■ **Gran Viale Santa Maria Elisabetta 21/B, Lido**

This well-stocked bike shop rents out all normal steeds as well as 4-wheeler family models.

⑥ Oviesse-Billa
MAP H2 ■ **Gran Viale Santa Maria Elisabetta 21/B, Lido**

A store with fashionable, moderately priced clothing for all ages, combined with a supermarket with a great selection of fresh produce for picnics.

⑦ Benetton
MAP H2 ■ **Gran Viale Santa Maria Elisabetta 47/B, Lido**

Despite being small, this store is well-stocked with underwear, nightwear and swimwear.

⑧ El Penelo
MAP F1 ■ **Palazzo Granaio Corso del Popolo, Chioggia**

Giorgio Boscolo is an expert on traditional fishermen's clay pipes – and he is the only craftsman who still makes them in terracotta and coloured glazes.

⑨ Venturini Souvenirs
MAP F1 ■ **Corso del Popolo 1349, Chioggia**

Ignore the trinkets here and instead focus on the intricately hand-crafted models of *bragozzo* boats (see p26).

Venturini Souvenirs

⑩ Panificio Sergio
MAP F1 ■ **Stradale Ponte Caneva 626, Chioggia**

The dry biscuits sold here were traditionally made for seafarers. *Pevarini* are spicy rings with molasses and aniseed, while *Dolce del Doge* is spread with a chocolate-hazelnut mixture.

Places to Eat

 Altanella
MAP E6 ▪ Calle delle Erbe, Giudecca 268 ▪ 041 522 77 80 ▪ Closed Mon & Tue, Dec & Jan, 10–20 Aug ▪ No disabled access ▪ €€€
Treat yourself to a candlelit dinner on the terrace. Fish dishes such as *frittura mista* (assorted fried seafood) are the speciality.

2 Ai Cacciatori
MAP D6 ▪ Fondamenta della Giudecca 320 ▪ 041 528 58 49 ▪ Closed Mon, 15 Dec–15 Jan ▪ €€€
Hearty Venetian fare such as *gnocchi con nero di seppia* (potato dumplings with cuttlefish ink) can be enjoyed in canal-side seating with lovely views.

3 Trattoria Scarso
MAP H2 ▪ Piazzale Malamocco 5, Malamocco ▪ 041 770 834 ▪ Closed Mon D, Tue, Jan, Nov ▪ €
This good-value family eatery has a lovely garden hung with fishing nets where you can linger over grilled fish or a fresh salad.

4 Trattoria La Favorita
MAP H2 ▪ Via Francesco Duodo 33, Lido ▪ 041 526 16 26 ▪ Closed Mon ▪ €€
This exemplary fish restaurant is a firm favourite with both locals and discerning visitors.

5 Trattoria Da Nane
Via Laguna 282, S Pietro in Volta ▪ 041 527 91 10 ▪ Closed Mon, mid-Nov–Easter ▪ No disabled access ▪ €€
Memorable fish restaurant with a terrace offering panoramic views. Its speciality is a fine *pasticcio di pesce* (seafood lasagne).

6 Ristorante da Memo
Via Portosecco 157, S Pietro in Volta ▪ 041 527 91 25 ▪ Closed Tue, Nov–Mar ▪ €€
A modest seafood restaurant with outdoor tables. Try the fresh shrimps, eel or sole.

Excellent view from Harry's Dolci

7 Harry's Dolci
MAP C6 ▪ S Eufemia, Giudecca 773 ▪ 041 522 48 44 ▪ Closed Mon D, Tue, Nov–Easter ▪ €€€
With views across the Giudecca Canal, this is the "sweet" branch of Harry's Bar (see p25), for sorbets and pastries.

8 Ristorante La Sgura
MAP F1 ▪ Fondamenta Marangoni 1295, Chioggia ▪ 041 403 232 ▪ Closed Mon, Jan ▪ €
In an enchanting setting on a quiet canal, this fish restaurant also has a great selection of meat. Try the *zuppa di pesce* (fish soup).

9 Ristorante El Gato
MAP F1 ▪ Corso del Popolo 653, Chioggia ▪ 041 400 265 ▪ Closed Mon & Tue, 15–28 Feb ▪ €€
Has an excellent and long-standing reputation for seafood; the *frittura* (fried fish), fish risotto and sautéed mussels and clams are a real treat.

10 Ristorante al Buon Pesce
MAP F1 ▪ Stradale Ponte Caneva 625, Chioggia ▪ 041 400 861 ▪ Closed Wed ▪ €
Spacious and friendly family-style fish restaurant with a delicious range of fresh grilled fish or fried seafood.

PRICE CATEGORIES

For a three-course meal for one with half a bottle of wine (or equivalent meal), taxes and extra charges.

€ under €40   €€ €40–60   €€€ over €60

See map on pp122–3 ➡

TOP 10 Padua, Vicenza and Verona

A wealth of art cities punctuates the fertile Veneto plain that stretches in a broad wedge north from the Po River to the foothills of the Dolomites. There is evidence of the presence of Romans and Venetians alike in the shape of fascinating amphitheatres and elegant palaces in places such as Verona and Vicenza, both recently declared World Heritage Sites by UNESCO. Moreover, amid vineyards of grapes pressed for light sparkling Prosecco and aromatic Bardolino are charming, little-visited villas with ornamental gardens. Each town has its distinctive character: business-like Padua, yet with a richly artistic and religious heart; Vicenza, contained and proper in its country setting and equally famous for its goldsmiths and Andrea Palladio's architecture; then romantic Verona, lazing on the banks of the mighty Adige River as it flows south swollen with snow-melt from the Alps. Highlights in each locality are all feasible as day-trips from Venice by train.

Piazza dei Signori

AREA MAP OF PADUA, VICENZA AND VERONA

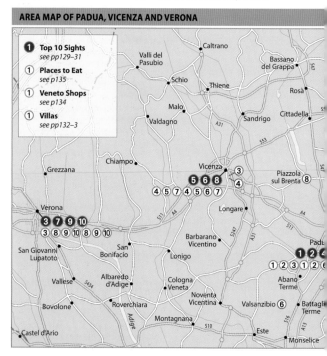

Top 10 Sights
see pp129–31

Places to Eat
see p135

Veneto Shops
see p134

Villas
see pp132–3

Fresco in the Cappella degli Scrovegni

1 Cappella degli Scrovegni
Piazza Eremitani, Padua
■ Bus Nos. 3, 10, 12 ■ 049 201
00 20 ■ Open 9am–7pm daily
■ Admission charge ■ www.
cappelladegliscrovegni.it

The sky-blue vault studded with gold stars in this glorious Paduan chapel seems to hover over Giotto's vibrant frescoes, which narrate the lives of Mary and Jesus. The Florentine artist (1266–1337) was summoned by Enrico Scrovegni to work on the chapel in 1305–6, to atone for the sins of his late father, a money-lender. Especially noteworthy among the 38 distinct scenes is the *Last Judgment* on the entrance wall, with its ranks of helmeted, haloed and shield-bearing angels. Book well in advance in summer. Visits last 30–35 minutes, including a 15-minute wait in the "decontamination" chamber.

2 Palazzo Bo
Via VIII Febbraio 2, Padua
■ Bus Nos. 3, 12 ■ 049 827 51 11
■ Guided tours on Mon, Wed & Fri am, Tue, Thu & Sat pm ■ Admission charge ■ www.unipd.it

The original lectern where Galileo Galilei held his lessons between 1592 and 1610 can be seen on the guided tour of Padua's historic university, founded in 1222 and second only to Bologna as Italy's oldest. The institution boasts the world's first anatomy theatre (1594) where dissections had to be carried out in great secrecy as the church forbade such practices. Other illustrious scholars of the university have included astronomer Copernicus (1473–1543), Gabriel Fallopius (1523–62), who discovered the function of the Fallopian tubes, and Elena Lucrezia Corner Piscopia, the world's first woman graduate *(see p44)*.

The 16th-century anatomy theatre in Padua's University

3 Casa di Giulietta

Via Cappello 23, Verona ▪ Open 8:30am–7:30pm Tue–Sun, 1:30–7:30pm Mon ▪ Admission charge

Tourists flock to "Juliet's House", the 13th-century presumed abode of the Shakespearean heroine, complete with a pretty balcony (added in 1928) from which you may imagine her uttering that immortal cry: "Romeo, Romeo, wherefore art thou Romeo?" The courtyard walls are filled with multilingual graffiti left by lovers from all over the world.

Juliet statue

4 Basilica del Santo

Piazza del Santo, Padua ▪ Bus Nos. 3, 18 ▪ Open 10am–6pm daily ▪ www.basilicadelsanto.org

Popularly referred to as "il Santo", Padua's revered site of pilgrimage was built in the 13th century to safeguard the mortal remains of St Anthony, a Franciscan monk and miracle worker from Portugal. Devotees visit his gleaming tomb, encircled by burning candles, but his tongue is guarded in an intricate reliquary in the Treasury, recovered after being stolen. Inside you will find artworks by Sansovino, Tiepolo and Titian (see p48–9).

5 Piazza dei Signori

Basilica Palladiana: Piazza dei Signori, Vicenza ▪ Open during exhibitions ▪ Admission charge

In addition to the cafés in Vicenza's main square, come to admire the buildings by Palladio, whose 16th-century designs went on to influence both his home town and architecture worldwide (see p49). The basilica boasts twin levels of colonnaded arches, opposite his Loggia del Capitaniato. A statue of the architect can be found in the piazzetta at the western end.

6 Palazzo Leoni Montanari

Contra' Santa Corona 25, Vicenza ▪ Open 10am–6pm Tue–Sun ▪ Admission charge

On the entrance portal of this lavishly decorated Baroque palace are carvings of writhing serpents, and Hercules is shown in the act of slaying the Hydra on the loggia. The gallery's masterpieces include 120 awe-inspiring Russian icons and 14 fascinating paintings by Pietro Longhi depicting scenes from 18th-century Venetian life.

7 Verona Arena

Piazza Brà, Verona ▪ 045 800 51 51 ▪ Open 8:30am–7:30pm Tue–Sun, 1:30–7:30pm Mon if no performance ▪ Limited wheelchair access ▪ Admission charge ▪ www.arena.it

This massive Roman amphitheatre from the 1st century AD measures almost 140 m (460 ft) in length. The arcades and 44-level tiered seating for 22,000 people, that once rang with the cries of gladiator fights, now echo with arias from operas during the popular summer festival. Verdi's *Aïda* has opened the festival every year since 1913. Visitors should note that the opening hours are shorter during the opera festival in the summer.

Verona Arena

8 Teatro Olimpico

Piazza Matteotti 11, Vicenza ▪ Open 9am–5pm Tue–Sun (Jul–Aug: 10am–6pm) ▪ Admission charge

A castle courtyard draped with creepers was chosen for this Vicenza theatre, designed by Palladio and completed by his disciple Vincenzo Scamozzi. The performing area is based on a Roman model, while the stage scenery represents the city of Thebes, built for 1585's inaugural play, Sophocles' *Oedipus Rex*. Scaled statues and varying stage levels create clever tricks of perspective.

Piazza delle Erbe in Verona

9 Piazza delle Erbe

Torre dei Lamberti, Cortile Mercato Vecchio, Verona ▪ Open Jun–Sep: 11am–7pm Tue–Sun; Oct–May: 9am–6pm Tue–Fri, 11am–7pm Sat–Sun ▪ Admission charge to the tower

Originally Verona's Roman forum, this square is still a great spot for discussing business over a coffee. Parasols shade souvenirs at the market, watched over by a winged lion atop a column, a vestige of Venetian domination. The 84-m (275-ft) Torre dei Lamberti offers great city views.

10 Museo di Storia Naturale

Lungadige Porta Vittoria 9, Verona ▪ Open 9am–5pm Mon–Thu; 2–6pm Sat & Sun ▪ Admission charge

Gigantic ferns, weird fish and an ancestor of the crocodile, all in fossilized form from the Eocene era 50 million years ago, are treasures hailing from Bolca in the Lessini foothills on display here. They testify to the tropical shallows that spread across the area prior to the formation of the Alps.

A DAY OUT IN VERONA

▶ **MORNING**

Where better to begin than the inspiring **Verona Arena**, where, as entertainment, wild animals once made a meal of gladiators? Afterwards, relax in the sun with a creamy coffee at **Liston 12 Caffè** and dig into a freshly baked jam-filled croissant *(Piazza Brà 12, Verona • 045 803 11 68)*.

A short stroll leads past the boutiques in the traffic-free **Via Mazzini**, paved with pink-tinged local limestone embedded with ammonite fossils, to **Casa di Giulietta** to the right, or **Piazza delle Erbe** and its elegant palaces to the left.

Backtrack to Via Mazzini for lunch at **Ristorante Greppia** *(Vicolo Samaritana 3, Verona • 045 800 45 77 • Closed Mon)* for *bollito misto* (mixed boiled meat) served with a traditional peppery sauce.

AFTERNOON

To digest lunch, head over the Adige River via the ancient **Ponte di Pietra** to the Roman theatre on Via Regaste Redentore – well worth a visit even if you're not in town for a summer evening performance. Then follow the river or walk back through town and west towards the medieval **Ponte Scaligero**, part of the adjoining castle. The triple-arched construction was blown up by the German army in World War II, then rebuilt brick by brick by town members.

The bridge leads to **Castelvecchio** for a timely *aperitivo* with a glass of white Soave wine at any of the welcoming bars.

See map on pp128–9 ◀

TOP 10 Veneto Villas

1 Villa Barbaro

Via Cornuda 7, Maser, bus from Treviso railway station ■ **Open Mar: 10:30am–6pm Tue, Thu & Sat, 11am–6pm Sun; Apr–Oct: 10am–6pm Tue–Sat, 11am–6pm Sun; Nov–Feb: 11am–5pm Sat & Sun** ■ **Admission charge** ■ **www.villadimaser.it**

The best preserved villa (1560) by Palladio (see p49) lies close to the pretty hill town of Asolo. This charming country house features all manner of Roman-inspired elements, from the nymphaeum and grotto to the circular temple akin to the Pantheon. Playful trompe l'oeil frescoes by Veronese (see p48) adorn the main rooms, while the garden is punctuated with Classical statuary. Drop in to the estate's wine cellar next door.

Villa Barbaro

rooms and a ballroom decorated by Tiepolo (see p48). Above the huge façade columns, scores of statues line the roof overlooking inner court-yards and a spacious park where the Venetian nobility would promenade on summer evenings. Be sure to explore the wonderful 1721 circular maze. The guest list has included one-time proprietor Napoleon, Russian and Austrian royalty, Mussolini and Hitler among others.

3 Villa Valmarana "Ai Nani"

Via dei Nani 8, Vicenza ■ **Open Mar–Oct: 10am–12:30pm, 3–6pm Tue–Fri, 10am–6pm Sat–Sun; Nov–Feb: 10am–12:30pm, 2–4pm Sat & Sun** ■ **Admission charge** ■ **www.villaval marana.com**

Known for the jaunty statues of dwarfs on the garden wall, these cosy twin buildings, built by the Valmarana family, stand on a pretty ridge looking up to Monte Berico and its sanctuary. The Tiepolo father and son fresco team were invited here by Count Valmarana in 1757 to decorate the main part and the guest quarters.

4 Villa Valmarana "La Rotonda"

Via Rotonda 45, Vicenza (bus No. 8) ■ **Open Mar–Oct: villa 10am–noon, 3–6pm Wed & Sat (Nov–Feb: 10am–noon, 2:30–5pm); garden open Tue–Sun same hours as villa** ■ **Admission charge** ■ **www.villalarotonda.it**

Perfectly proportioned imposing villa with four temple façades on a hill overlooking the architect Palladio's adoptive town of Vicenza. The house has been imitated throughout the world. If you want to visit the villa itself as opposed to the rather limited grounds, beware: it's only open two days a week.

Villa Pisani – La Nazionale

2 Villa Pisani – La Nazionale

Via Doge Pisani 7, Strà ■ **Villa & park: open 9am–7pm Tue–Sun (Oct–Mar: 9am–4pm); maze: open Apr–Oct** ■ **Admission charge** ■ **www.villapisani.beniculturali.it**

A splendid two-floor 18th-century villa designed for Doge Alvise Pisani, with 114 sumptuously furnished

5 Villa Foscari "La Malcontenta"
Via dei Turisti 9, Malcontenta ▪ Open May–Oct: 9am–noon Tue & Sat ▪ Adm charge ▪ www.lamalcontenta.com
Wonderful residence on the bend of the Brenta Canal, but now rather too close to the Marghera industrial area. Designed by Andrea Palladio in 1571, it is one of his best-known creations, with a Greek temple façade, while the interior is decorated with frescoes. The name is said to refer to the "discontent" of a female member of the Foscari family, exiled here for adultery.

6 Villa Barbarigo
Galzignano, Valsanzibio ▪ Open Mar–Nov: 10am–1pm, 2pm–sunset daily ▪ Admission charge ▪ www.valsanzibiogiardino.it
The Euganean Hills are the setting for this Baroque garden, designed for the Venetian Barbarigo family by Luigi Bernini, architect of the Vatican fountains in Rome. The villa, dating from 1669, is a private dwelling, but the 15-ha (37-acre) garden provides a boxwood maze, fountains, fish ponds, statues and hundreds of trees.

7 Villa Emo
Via Stazione 5, Fanzolo di Vedelago ▪ Open May–Oct: 3–7pm Mon–Sat, 9:30am–12:30pm, 3–7pm Sun; Nov–Apr: 10am–12:30pm, 2:30–5:30pm Mon–Sat, 9am–12:30pm, 2–6pm Sun ▪ Admission charge ▪ www.villaemo.org
Another of Palladio's light-flooded country residences, built for the Emo family in around 1560. A harmonious central block is flanked by graceful arched *barchesse* (wings), designed for storing hay and farm tools. The interior has lively frescoes by Renaissance artist Zelotti, also responsible for the Malcontenta villa decorations.

8 Villa Contarini
Piazzola sul Brenta ▪ Open Mar–Oct: 9am–7pm Thu–Tue; Nov–Feb: 10am–4pm Thu–Tue ▪ Adm charge ▪ www.villacontarini.eu
A horseshoe plaza lined with terraced houses faces the façade of this 17th-century country villa, which was once the focus for a thriving farming community. A remarkable system of acoustics was invented so that musicians performing in the Sala della Musica on the first floor could be clearly heard and appreciated downstairs. An antiques market is held in the grounds on the last Sunday of each month.

9 Villa Cornaro
Via Roma 35, Piombino Dese ▪ Open May–Sep: 3:30–6pm Sat ▪ Admission charge
This unusual, double-tiered, compact Palladio creation dates back to between 1560 and 1570. The façade columns are both Doric and Corinthian in style, with acanthus leaves or scrolls around the capitals.

10 Barchessa Valmarana
Via Valmarana 11, Mira ▪ Open Mar–Oct: 10am–6pm Tue–Sun ▪ Admission charge ▪ www.villavalmarana.net
Formerly guest quarters, these are extant "wings" of a 17th-century villa, whose main body was demolished in 1908. Close by are locks on the Brenta waterway, which have been excavated over centuries to divert the river away from the lagoon and eliminate the problem of silting.

Beautiful interior of Villa Emo

See map on pp128–9

Veneto Shops

1 Pasticceria Gelateria Al Duomo
Via Vandelli 2, Padua ■ **Closed Tue**

This pastry shop has been serving up the finest *fritelle* (apple fritters) in town for many decades. It is located on the southern corner of the square by the Duomo.

2 Drogheria ai Due Catini d'Oro
Piazza dei Frutti 46, Padua

This old-fashioned shop sells super-strong mints, peppery Veneto *mostarda* chutney and even feather dusters, among many other things.

3 Boutique Novella
Via C Cattaneo 18, Verona

Everything for the female fashionista, created by top Italian designers.

4 Antica Pasticceria di Sorarù
Piazzetta Palladio 17, Vicenza

This inviting pastry shop is lined with tantalizing almond and chocolate delicacies, as well as special goodies such as the dove-shaped *colomba* cake at Easter.

Antica Pasticceria di Sorarù

5 Cappelleria Palladio
Piazzetta Palladio 13, Vicenza

Hat-lovers' heaven, run by a charming couple with a 40-year passion for millinery in this lovely old-fashioned establishment. In great demand for stylish weddings in the country villas *(see pp132–3)*.

6 Feltrinelli Internazionale
Via S Francesco 7, Padua

You could occupy yourself for hours by browsing the well-stocked shelves of English- and other European-language crime and mystery novels, fiction, travel, classics, children's literature and reference books in this chain bookshop.

7 Il Ceppo
Corso Palladio 196, Vicenza

A gourmet's paradise with mouthwatering takeaway dishes, pickles and preserves. Buy a catered picnic with wine or simply a crusty roll filled with Asiago cheese or *sopressa* sausage.

8 De Rossi "Il Fornaio"
Corso Porta Borsari 3, Verona

A range of pastries and wholemeal breads is available here. Try the *zaletto*, a biscuit baked with pine nuts and sultanas, and of course *Baci di Giulietta* (Juliet's Kisses) – almond paste shaped into pursed lips.

9 Mercante d'Oriente
Corso Sant'Anastasia 34, Verona

Akin to an exotic museum, this antiques dealer dazzles with Chinese and Japanese marvels, Pre-Columbian pieces and traditional and contemporary carpets.

10 Coin
Via Cappello 30, Verona

This wonderful department store, with a good range of casual clothes, cosmetics and home furnishings, is right in the centre of town.

Places to Eat

1 Graziati
Piazza della Frutta 40, Padua
■ €

Light and buttery *millefoglie* pastries perfectly accompany the strong, sweet coffee as you sit outside on the lively market square. Light lunches are served downstairs.

2 Caffè Pedrocchi
Via VIII Febbraio 15, Padua ■ €

This 1831 Neo-Classical coffee house was long known as the "café without doors" because it never closed. Liberals of the 19th century would meet and argue here, though today it's rather quiet.

Caffè Pedrocchi

3 Osteria dei Fabbri
Via dei Fabbri 13, Padua
■ 049 650 33 62 ■ Closed Sun ■ €

The appetizing menu in this rustic *osteria* changes daily, so you may get grilled Piedmont cheese with polenta or spare ribs with *radicchio* (chicory).

4 Antico Guelfo
Contrà Pedemuro San Biagio 90, Vicenza ■ 0444 547 897
■ Closed Sun ■ €€

This central, upmarket restaurant offers more than the usual fare, including superb gluten-free cuisine. The restaurant also has an excellent selection of wines. Great value.

5 Antica Casa della Malvasia
Contrà delle Morette 5, Vicenza
■ 0444 543 704 ■ Closed Sun dinner, Mon, 2 weeks in Jul ■ €

There is an imaginative menu and vast wine list here. Try the *bigoli all'arna* (spaghetti with duck sauce).

6 Piccadilly Cafe
Contrà Daniele Manin 20, Vicenza ■ 340 267 67 75 ■ Closed Wed ■ €

Lively bar serving great cocktails, bar snacks and a wide variety of beers. There's outdoor seating in Piazza dei Signori.

7 Angolo Palladio
Piazzetta Palladio 12, Vicenza ■ 0444 327 790 ■ Closed Thu lunch ■ €€

This warm and friendly pizzeria-cum-restaurant serves excellent *baccalà* (salt cod) and boasts an extensive wine list.

8 Ristorante Greppia
Vicolo Samaritana 3, Verona
■ 045 800 45 77 ■ Closed Mon, 1–15 Jun ■ €

An unforgettable place specializing in *bollito misto*, a selection of nine melt-in-the-mouth meats served with peppery *Pearà* sauce.

9 Arche
Via Arche Scaligere 6, Verona
■ 045 800 74 15 ■ Closed Mon lunch, Sun dinner, 2 weeks in Jan ■ €–€€€

Established in 1879, this is one of the best restaurants in Verona. Fish dishes feature strongly on the menu.

10 Bottega del Vino
Vicolo Scudo di Francia 3, Verona ■ 045 800 45 35 ■ €€

Renowned restaurant that dates back to 1890 and holds 2,500 wines in its cellar. Food-wise, the favourite for aficionados is *pastissada de caval*, a dark, spicy horse-meat stew.

See map on pp128–9

Streetsmart

Colourful canal houses on Burano

Getting To and Around Venice

Arriving by Air

Marco Polo, Venice's main airport, is located 10 km (6.5 miles) north of the city, at the edge of the lagoon. It is served by many European airlines, including **British Airways** and low-cost easyJet and Jet2, whereas the national carrier **Alitalia** flies via Rome. London, Amsterdam, Frankfurt and Paris are also transport hubs for Venice. From the United States, **Delta Airlines** flies direct from New York, and American Airways flies direct from Philadelphia.

The most exciting way to reach Venice from the airport is by water. The public Alilaguna **water bus** (vaporetto) leaves every 15 minutes and takes about an hour. Tickets (€15) are available at the nearby quayside. A **water taxi** (motoscafo) takes about half the time but will cost around €110. The cheaper option is to take a bus to Piazzale Roma. The direct **ATVO shuttle bus** (€8) and the **ACTV public bus** No. 5 (€8) leave every 30 minutes. There is a ticket office in the arrivals hall.

Charter flights and the low-cost airline Ryanair fly into Antonio Canova Airport at **Treviso**, which is 40 km (29 miles) northwest of Venice. To reach Venice from here, you can take an ATVO shuttle bus to Piazzale Roma (€10), which takes around 50 mins, or the public bus No. 6 (€1.30) to Treviso station and then continue by train.

Arriving by Sea

Ferries and cruise ships from Greece and Croatia dock at the **Venezia Terminal Passeggeri** near Tronchetto or the San Basilio terminal in western Dorsoduro.

Arriving by Train

Stazione Venezia Santa Lucia is the terminus for trains from the major European cities. Passengers from London need to change in Paris or Ostend. Vaporetti connect with all parts of the city from here. Don't make the mistake of getting out at Venezia Mestre, the stop before Venice itself. Travelling by the Venice Simplon-Orient-Express from London is a romantic, albeit very costly, way to arrive.

Arriving by Coach

Long-distance and international coaches such as **Eurolines** arrive at Tronchetto, which is four minutes from Piazzale Roma on the People Mover railway shuttle (€1.50).

Arriving by Road

If you come from an EEA/EU country, you will need a valid driving licence and credit card to hire a car. Otherwise an International Driving Licence is necessary. If you are driving your own car, bring vehicle registration papers and full insurance cover. Italians drive on the right. Since no cars are allowed in Venice, you will need to leave your car in one of the large car parks on the outskirts or at the airport. Those nearest the city, on Tronchetto or at Piazzale Roma, are more expensive than those at Fusina and San Giuliano near Mestre. The only reason to hire a car from Venice would be to explore the Veneto, but Padua, Vicenza and Verona are all easily accessible on a day-trip by train or bus. Car hire is available at Piazzale Roma and the airport.

Getting Around on Foot

Venice is a compact city – crossing from north to south only takes around 45 minutes – and, aided by the excellent network of vaporetti, which also travel to the outlying islands, it's easy to see the main sights on foot. Four bridges cross the Grand Canal.

It is also a city where getting lost in the tangle of alleyways (calli) is part of the attraction. Arming yourself with a detailed street map will help you get around, as will the frequent yellow signs on the walls indicating the direction of the main sights. The etiquette of walking is to keep to the right and to keep moving on bridges or in the narrowest alleyways. Once you are out of the San Marco and Rialto districts, however, the flow of tourists becomes much less. The alleyways open out into numerous squares *(campi)* with benches and cafés.

Getting Around by Water

Vaporetti cross and travel the length of the Grand Canal, and are the equivalent of buses in Venice. The most useful route, Line No. 1, makes a leisurely journey (45 minutes) down the Grand Canal from Piazzale Roma to San Marco. Line No. 2 is the Canal's faster route; and Line 12, from Fondamente Nuove, serves the islands of Murano, Burano and Torcello. The service is run by ACTV, and tickets are available at boarding points, bars and tobacconists. There is a flat one-way fare (€7.50), no matter how far you travel. It is important to validate your ticket on the electronic reader before you board, or you may be liable to a hefty fine; you must then start your journey within one hour. Be aware that the stops serve both directions. Most lines run 5am–midnight, and there is a limited night service. You can buy an ACTV travel card for 1, 2, 3 or 7 days, which you can also load on to the **Venezia Unica City Pass**.

There are 16 water-taxi ranks from where sleek motor boats *(motoscafi)* provide the fastest – but not cheapest – way of getting around. Luggage and waiting cost extra.

Easily recognizable gondoliers await business at the numerous **gondola** ranks. Official rates are €80 for 40 minutes by day,

and €100 by night, but establish a price before setting out. Gondolas can take up to six passengers.

Traghetti, gondola ferries with an oarsman at each end, cross the Grand Canal (€2) at eight points in daylight. Most residents travel standing up.

Getting Around by Bicycle

Bicycles are banned from the centre, but you can hire a bike for trips on the Lido and Pellestrina, and for excursions out of Venice. **Veloce** arrange customized excursions.

DIRECTORY

AIRPORTS

Treviso, Antonio Canova
- 042 231 51 11
- w trevisoairport.it

Venice, Marco Polo
- 041 260 92 60
- w veniceairport.it

AIRLINES

Alitalia
- w alitalia.com

British Airways
- w britishairways.com

Delta Airlines
- w delta.com

CRUISE AND FERRY TERMINAL

Venezia Terminal Passeggeri
- w vtp.it

TRAINS

Venice Simplon-Orient-Express
- w belmond.com/venice-simplon-orient-express/

Trenitalia
- 89 20 21 or 39 06 684 754 75 from abroad
- w trenitalia.com

COACHES

Eurolines
- w eurolines.com

ROAD INFORMATION

ACI (Italian Automobile Club)
- w aci.it

CAR HIRE

Europcar
- w europcar.it

Maggiore
- w maggiore.it

BUSES

ACTV
- 041 24 24
- w actv.it

ATVO
- 0421 59 44
- w atvo.it

WATER TRANSPORT

ACTV
- w actv.it

Alilaguna
- 041 240 17 01
- w alilaguna.it

Gondolas
- 041 528 50 75
- w gondolavenezia.it

Water Buses *(Vaporetti)*
- 041 2424

Water Taxis *(Motoscafi)*
Consorzio Motoscafi
- 041 522 23 03
- w motoscafivenezia.it

Consorzio Venezia Taxi
- 041 723 009
- w veneziataxi.it

Cooperitiva Taxi Serenissima
- 041 522 12 65
- w serenissimataxi.it

BICYCLE

Veloce
- w rentalbikeitaly.com

TICKETS AND PASSES

Venezia Unica
- 041 24 24
- w veneziaunica.it

Practical Information

Passports and Visas

All visitors to Italy need a valid passport. For residents of the European Union (EU), European Economic Area (EEA), Switzerland, United States, Canada, Australia, New Zealand and Israel visas are only required for stays in excess of 90 days or for those intending to work, but check with your embassy before travelling. Contact your consulate if you lose your passport, need a visa or wish to stay longer than 90 days.

Customs Information

Allowances for visitors from the EU are almost unlimited, if for personal use only. If you need medication, bring enough to last your visit and a copy of your prescription. Check ahead for allowances within and without the EU on the Travel Visa Services website.

Travel Safety Advice

Visitors can get up-to-date travel safety information from the **Foreign and Commonwealth Office** in the UK, the **State Department** in the US and the **Department of Foreign Affairs and Trade** in Australia.

Travel Insurance

It's advisable to take out an insurance policy to cover cancellation or curtailment of your trip, theft, loss of money and baggage, and healthcare, including repatriation. Visitors from EU/EEA countries should bring a European Health Insurance Card (EHIC) which will give free or reduced healthcare including pre-existing medical conditions and routine maternity care, but will not cover repatriation.

Health

For urgent medical aid, go to the emergency (pronto soccorso) department of the **SS. Giovanni e Paolo Hospital** in Castello. If you need an ambulance (ambulanza), dial 118. There are First Aid Points for tourists, open 8am to 8pm daily, in Piazza San Marco and Piazzale Roma. The **Health Venice** website lists doctors and pharmacies, and your hotel or a tourist office can supply contact numbers for night doctors and dentists.

Pharmacies (farmacie) tend to open 9am–12.30pm and 4–7.30pm Monday to Friday, and 9am–noon on Saturdays. A rota (farmacie di turno) of night-time and Sunday opening is posted on pharmacy doors. The Un Ospite di Venezia booklet (see p143) also has this information. Italian pharmacists are trained to deal with minor ailments.

No inoculations are needed. Take a high-factor sunscreen in summer. An insect repellent and an electric plug-in insect killer will help guard against mosquitoes. It is safe to drink tap water and water from fountains unless you see the sign non potabile (not drinkable).

Personal Security

Venice is a safe city, but still has its share of pickpockets. Leave important documents and valuables in a hotel safe and only carry the money you need Be extra vigilant at train stations, markets, on public transport, at the landing stages of the vaporetti – especially while boarding. Venice is safe at night, and women alone should encounter no trouble. Make sure you only use official taxis, or you may be overcharged.

In the event of a theft, report it at the nearest police station (questura) and take your passport. But if you have lost your passport, consult your consulate immediately. In any emergency, call 112 for assistance (pronto soccorso); or call 113 for the police (Polizia di Stato) or 115 for the fire brigade (Vigili del Fuoco). Items left on vaporetti are kept at the **ACTV Lost Property** (Oggetti Smarriti) offices (7:30am–7:30pm daily) in Piazzale Roma for a week.

Disabled Travellers

For travellers in wheel-chairs, the Venezia Accessibile information pack, available online or at tourist offices, details the best way of getting around the 70 per cent of Venice that is wheelchair accessible. It lists barrier-free itineraries, arrangements for arriving by train, air and bus, public toilets, car parks, manageable bridges and travelling by vaporetto or motoscafo.

The website also lists shops where one can hire lightweight wheelchairs. Wheelchair users can buy discounted single-fare tickets for the *vaporetti*, which last 75 minutes and allow a companion to travel free.

Museums and churches are usually free for wheelchair users and companions; call ahead or check with the tourist office for details. Booking and specialist websites, such as www.europeforvisitors. com, list hotels that are suitable for the disabled. The **Sage Travel** website is packed with detailed information. **Can Be Done** specializes in holidays and tailor-made packages for the disabled.

Senior Travellers

Senior travellers are eligible for reduced fees to churches and museums. You will need photographic ID as proof of age. If you are planning to travel by train, it's worth buying the *carta d'argento*, which gives over-60s a 15 per cent discount. A yearly card costs €30 (free to over-75s) and is available at stations and travel agencies or online.

Students and Young People

Students should bring an **International Student Identity Card (ISIC)** card with them for reduced fares and entry fees. Those aged 14 to 29 can get a **Venezia Unica** card (€4) for a 72-hour pass (€20) on public transport and other discounts.

Travelling with Children

Family passes are available for the *vaporetti*, museums and churches. Children under 6 travel free on public transport, and discounted or free entry to sights come with the Chorus Pass (under 11) and Museum Pass (under 6; see p143). Parks and the Lido beaches offer respite from churches and museums. Most restaurants will have children's meals. Bring a lightweight pushchair, as negotiating the bridges can be tiring.

DIRECTORY

PASSPORTS AND VISAS

Italian Foreign Office
W esteri.it

Travel Visa and Passport Services
W italy.visahq.com

EMBASSIES AND CONSULATES

Australia
Via Borgogna 2, Milan
C 02 7767 4200
W italy.embassy.gov.au

Canada
Via Zara 30, Rome
C 06 854 442 911 (24hrs)
W canadainternational. gc.ca

New Zealand
Via Terraggio 17, Milan
C 02 721 70001
W nzembassy.com/italy

United Kingdom
Via San Paolo 7, Milan
C 02 723 001 (24 hrs)
W gov.uk/government/ world/italy

United States
Via Principe Amadeo 2/10, Milan
C 02 290 351
W milan.usconsulate.gov

CUSTOMS

Customs Information
W visahq.com

TRAVEL SAFETY ADVICE

Australia
Department of Foreign Affairs and Trade
W dfat.gov.au/ smartraveller.gov.au

United Kingdom
Foreign and Commonwealth Office
W gov.uk/foreign-travel-advice

United States
US Department of State
W travel.state.gov

HEALTH

Health Venice
W healthvenice.com

Ospedale SS Giovanni e Paolo
MAP F3 ■ Castello 6777
C 118 (for emergencies)

PERSONAL SECURITY

Questura
MAP B3 ■ Fondamente di S Chiara, Santa Croce, 500
C 041 271 55 86

ACTV Lost Property
MAP B3 ■ Garage Communale, Piazzale Roma
C 041 272 21 79

City Lost Property
MAP P4 ■ Ca' Farsetti, San Marco 4136
C 041 274 82 25

DISABLED TRAVELLERS

Accessible Venice
W comune.venezia.it/

Sage Travel
W sagetraveling.com

Can Be Done
W canbedone.co.uk

Wheelchair Transport

Sanitrans
C 041 523 99 77
W sanitrans.net

STUDENTS

International Student Identity Card
W isic.org

Venezia Unica
W veneziaunica.it

TRAVELLING WITH CHILDREN
W travelforkids.com

Currency and Banking

Italy uses the euro, the common currency of the European Union. Bank notes come in seven denominations – 5, 10, 20, 50, 100, 200 and 500 – and coins, eight: 1, 2, 5, 10, 20 and 50 cents, plus €1 and €2. There is no limit on the amount of cash you can bring into the country.

Banks are usually open 8:30am—1:30pm Monday to Friday and close at weekends and public holidays. Almost all banks have a cashpoint or ATM (*bancomat*), which displays the logos of the cards they accept, as well as giving multilingual instructions. Be careful to shield your PIN, which should consist of four digits only. It's worth checking whether you need to inform your bank that you will be making foreign withdrawals before you leave. You should also find out the rate of commission and transaction charges. All major credit and debit cards (Mastercard, Visa, American Express) are widely accepted in Italy's hotels, restaurants and shops. If you lose a card or have it stolen, report it immediately on the appropriate emergency number from your provider.

Foreign-exchange offices are open seven days a week, but commission rates tend to be high. Those at Venice's train station and airport stay open until the evening and at weekends. Post offices offer the same service.

Telephone and Internet

Tri-band and GSM mobile phones will work in Italy, but confirm the roaming charges before you leave. The alternative – if your mobile can be unlocked – is to buy an Italian pay-as-you-go SIM card from **TIM**, **Wind** or **Vodafone**. Top-ups are available from tobacconists (*tabacchi*) and news-stands, where you can also buy phonecards (*carte telefoniche*) for public phone boxes. When calling an Italian landline, it must be prefixed by its full area code even within the city you are calling from, and the 0 must be kept when dialling an Italian number from abroad. To call Venice from abroad, dial the access code 00 39 (0 11 39 from the US and Canada, 00 11 39 from Australia), followed by the 041 city code. Mobile numbers begin with 3 and are not prefixed by a 0. Skype (www.skype.com) is the cheapest option for international calls.

Internet and Wi-Fi is widely available in hotels, some restaurants and cafés. You can buy access to the municipal Venice Wi-Fi network for 24hrs, 72hrs or a week through the Venezia Unica card, though this focuses on the main squares and thoroughfares.

Postal Services

Stamps (*francobolli*) can be bought at post offices and *tabacchi*, which are recognizable by the black-and-white "T" sign. Post offices are open Monday to Saturday, mornings only, but the central office in San Marco is open all day. You can find a complete list with opening hours on the Italian Post website. Use the *Posta Prioritaria* service if you want letters to arrive quickly.

TV, Radio and Newspapers

Beside the three state TV channels – RAI 1, RAI 2 and RAI 3 – satellite and cable TV transmit foreign channels such as CNN, Sky News, and the BBC World Service in many languages. The main radio stations – Radio 1, Radio 2 and Radio 3 – are also run by RAI. Venice Classic Radio (www.veniceclassic-radio.eu) and La Fenice Radio (www.lafenice.radio.net) both stream Italian classical music.

European and US newspapers are sold at large newsagents a day or so after publication. Local daily newspapers such as *Il Gazzettino* and *La Nuova Venezia* are useful for event listings, as is the national daily *Corriere della Sera*.

Opening Hours

Many museums are open daily, but times are subject to change, so it is wise to check. The main churches are usually open 10am–5pm Monday to Saturday. Food shops are open 9am–1pm and 4–7.30pm Monday to Saturday, except for Wednesday afternoon. In low season, clothing and gift stores close all day Sunday and also Monday mornings.

Public Holidays

Venice observes the following public holidays: New Year's Day (1 Jan), Epiphany (6 Jan), Easter Monday (variable), Liberation Day and St Mark's Day (both celebrated on 25 Apr) Labour Day (1 May), Republic Day (2 Jun), Assumption (15 Aug), All Saints' Day (1 Nov), Salute (21 Nov), Immaculate Conception (8 Dec), Christmas Day (25 Dec), Boxing Day (26 Dec).

Time Difference

Italy is one hour ahead of Greenwich Mean Time (GMT) and changes to Daylight Saving Time (ora legale) from the Last Sunday in March to the last Sunday in October, putting the country two hours ahead of GMT. For all official purposes, Italy uses the 24-hour clock.

Electrical Appliances

The electrical current in Italy is 220V AC with two-pin, round-pronged plugs. Bring a travel adapter for electrical appliances.

Weather

Every season in Venice has its attractions, but July and August can get very hot (up to 28° C/ 82° F) and sticky. Spring and autumn are cooler (around 15° C/59° F). Between October and March, Venice often experiences acqua alta (tidal flooding), which spreads out from Piazza San Marco. Sirens give an alert to an impending

flood, and a network of passerelle (wooden walkways) are erected on the main routes around the city. You can buy plastic overshoes and find details on tide height on the municipal website.

Tourist Information

There are official tourist offices, Azienda di Promozione Turistica, (APT) at the airport, in Piazza San Marco, Santa Lucia train station and at Piazzale Roma, which provide city and vaporetto maps and other information. The free monthly magazine Un Ospite di Venezia – published in English as A Guest in Venice – gives listings, useful practical information, and boat timetables and is widely distributed in hotels. Look out, too, for wall posters advertising local festivities and cultural events. You can also pick up details of what's on from the tourist offices, or consult the websites below. If you intend visiting a number of churches, consider a Chorus Pass (€12), which gives entry to 18 churches and organizes guided tours. (Single entrance to churches costs €3.) Though you are not required to cover your head, it is important to dress respectfully when visiting churches and avoid bare arms, shorts and beachwear. The Museum Pass (€24.50) allows entry to 11 museums. The most comprehensive pass, however, is the Venezia Unica city pass (see p141), which you can

tailor to your needs. It gives access to museums, churches, vaporetti, public toilets and Wi-Fi. It is also available at various points around the city.

DIRECTORY

TELEPHONE SERVICES

TIM
📞 041 523 12 62
🌐 tim.it

Vodafone
📞 041 296 01 43
🌐 vodafone.it

Wind
📞 049 261 06 54
🌐 wind.it

POSTAL SERVICES
🌐 poste.it

Main Post Office
MAP P3 ▪ Calle Larga de L'Ascension, San Marco 1241

WEATHER
🌐 ilmeteo.it

Acqua Alta Information
🌐 comune.venezia.it/ maree

TOURIST INFORMATION

APT
📞 041 529 87 11
🌐 turismovenezia.it

LISTINGS

La Biennale di Venezia
🌐 labiennale.org

Un Ospite di Venezia
🌐 unospitedivenezia.it

PASSES

Chorus Pass
📞 041 275 04 62
🌐 chorusvenezia.org

Museum Pass
🌐 visitmuve.it

WEBSITES
🌐 turismovenezia.it
🌐 venezia.net
🌐 venezia.travel
🌐 veniceforyou.com
🌐 visit-venice-italy.com

Shopping

Venice has myriad fascinating shops, a selection of which has been picked out for inclusion in each district in this book. Glass and beads, masks, handmade paper and paper goods, lace and gondolier hats are all popular souvenir items with tourists.

When buying glassware, it is worth shopping around: many glass shops stock similar items, and prices can vary wildly. Murano tends to be more expensive than Venice, but you get a free demonstration as well. Make sure you can see the authentic Vetro Artistico® Murano trademark before buying anything that is claimed to be from Murano. Virtually all glass-shop staff are experts in packaging fragile and bulky items, and they can arrange for forwarding overseas by air or sea. Always check that insurance is included. Visitors from non-EU countries can claim a tax refund on purchases that exceed €155 from one shop. Most shopkeepers will have the appropriate forms.

The Mercerie – the district that joins the Rialto Bridge to Piazza San Marco – has a concentration of high-end stores such as Dolce & Gabbana, Prada and Armani selling designer clothing, shoes and handbags. Calle Larga XXII Marzo also has a cluster of chic shops. In the Cannaregio district, **Coin**, the only department store in Venice, stocks upmarket designer brands and is open every day of the week.

Delicatessen, bakeries and specialist shops are centred around the Rialto Market, where you can find enticing displays of fresh produce. For food shopping, there are a number of supermarkets throughout the city – Coop Adriatica, Conad and Punto, for instance – which stay open late and on Sundays. Note that shopkeepers are obliged by law to give you a receipt. Street sellers do a brisk trade in tourist bric-à-brac, as well as imitation designer bags and accessories. However, be warned that hefty fines are imposed for anyone who is caught buying counterfeit goods.

Dining

Restaurant opening hours are generally 12:30–2:30pm and 7–10pm. Venice caters mainly to tourists, often on a day trip, so the further you venture from the main tourist spots, the less likely you are to find a *menu turistico* and waiters luring you in, and the more likely you are to discover good Venetian cuisine. It's best to book ahead as restaurants are often small. The cover charge *(coperto)* of around €2 and a service charge *(servizio)* of up to 12 per cent should be indicated clearly on the menu and also on the bill.

Venetians often take an early evening *giro all'ombra* (stroll in the shade), which involves eating *cicheti* (snacks) with wine, in various local *bacari* (small bars). The classic Venetian *aperitivo* is a spritz – a mixture of white wine, Aperol and sparkling mineral water.

Because the city is situated between a lagoon and the sea, plenty of fish appears on restaurant menus – Venetian specialities include baby cuttlefish cooked in its own ink and eel cooked in Marsala wine. Look out for traditional *bigoli* (a long thick, dark pasta), *frittelle alla Veneziane* (fried sweet doughnuts with lemon and Marsala) and the almond confectionery *torrone*. Burano residents are proud of their *bussolai* – ring-shaped cinnamon-flavoured biscuits. Italians never drink a cappuccino after lunch or dinner, instead choosing an espresso or a *digestivo*.

Pizza places are less expensive than restaurants, as is the self-service Brek chain. For something more substantial, find a *tavola calda* (cafeteria), where hot meals are served at a counter. Vegetarian restaurants are a rarity – Le Spighe in Castello is one *(see p113)* – but you can find vegetarian choices at many restaurants.

Drinking coffee in bars while standing up, as the locals do, will cost you half as much as sitting at a table. The ultimate, albeit ultra-expensive, coffee experience is sitting at either Caffè Florian or Quadri's in "Europe's drawing room" of Piazza San Marco *(see pp20–21)*, while an orchestra plays and you simply watch the world go by.

Note that smoking is prohibited in bars,

restaurants and all public indoor places, though electronic cigarettes are permitted. Picnicking on bridges, church steps or in Piazza San Marco is also not welcomed. Look for a bench in one of the squares or parks instead, and eat discreetly.

Trips and Tours

The official tour guides (**Cooperativa Guide Turistiche Autorizzate**) can give you in-depth history and history-of-art background for every corner of Venice in 15 different languages. Tours with English-speaking guides can be booked through tourist offices and agencies such as **A Guide in Venice** and **Bucintoro Viaggi**, which also organizes gondola rides, working out more affordably if you are part of a group.

You can learn to row like a gondolier with qualified English-speaking instructors with **Row Venice**. Prices start at €40 per person.

Private tours of some of Venice's museums can be combined with historical walking tours through **Venice Museums**, and the **Jewish Museum** offers a guided tour of three of the synagogues in the Ghetto Nuovo (see p103). They can also arrange tours of the old Jewish cemetery on the Lido (see p123).

Outside of Venice, you can spend a full day or half a day cruising the Brenta Canal on the motorboat **Il Burchiello**, which includes visiting the Palladian villas, once the summer residences of Venetian nobility. The return journey from Padua is made by bus.

Where to Stay

Venice's hotels cater for every budget, although being mainly small (20 rooms or fewer), they book up quickly. It's wise to book as far ahead as you can and to look for special deals online. Spaces fill up quickly at Carnival time in February or early March, as well as for the Film Festival in September. The Venice Biennale is held in odd-numbered years and also puts an extra strain on accommodation.

Hotels nearest Piazza San Marco are the most expensive, and a view of a canal costs more. The Lido and mainland Mestre are less expensive but can be noisier, since they are not traffic-free. Northern Cannaregio and eastern Castello are quiet areas; Dorsoduro has more bars and nightlife. There is also a good choice of guesthouses, bed and breakfasts, hostels and even camping sites. Apartments and house exchanges are another possibility to consider.

Travel for Kids has an extensive list of apartments and hotels that are suitable for families. **Truly Venice** offers luxury apartments, with plenty for larger groups.

Rates and Booking

Prices are by room, and it's wise to check whether breakfast is included. Hotel prices are generally low between early November and Easter and high during the Carnival period from February to March. Some hotels are also cheaper in July and August, when the city can get very humid. A couple of important points to consider when booking are the distance you will have to walk from the *vaporetto* stop and the amount of luggage you will be carrying; it's best kept to a minimum, since porters are expensive. Cases on wheels should be carried over bridges.

DIRECTORY

SHOPPING

Coin Department Store
W coin.it

TRIPS AND TOURS

A Guide in Venice
W info@aguidein venice.com
W aguideinvenice.com

Bucintoro Viaggi
C 041 521 06 32
W bucintoroviaggi.com

Cooperative Tour Guides of Venice (Cooperativa Guide Turistiche Autorizzate)
C 041 520 90 38
W guidevenezia.it

Il Burchiello
C 049 876 02 33
W ilburchiello.it

Jewish Museum
W museoebraico.it

Row Venice
C 340 341 3448
W rowvenice.org

Venice Museums
W venice-museum.com

WHERE TO STAY

Booking Agencies
Home Exchange
W homeexchange.com

Travel for Kids
W travelforkids.com

Truly Venice
W trulyvenice apartments.com

Places to Stay

PRICE CATEGORIES

For a standard, double room per night (with breakfast if included), taxes and extra charges.

€ under €150   €€ €150–350   €€€ over €350

Luxury Hotels

Grand Hotel Palazzo dei Dogi

MAP D1 ■ Fondamenta Madonna dell'Orto, Cannaregio 35 00 ■ 041 220 81 11 ■ www. boscolohotels.com ■ €€
With a lovely garden stretching back to the lagoon, this former convent on a quiet Cannaregio canal is furnished with Murano chandeliers and fabrics crafted by leading artisans. Best-value luxury hotel in town, with its own guest launch.

Aman Venice

MAP N3 ■ San Polo 1364 ■ 041 270 73 33 ■ www. aman.com ■ No disabled access ■ €€€
The hotel launch brings guests from the airport to the Grand Canal entrance to Palazzo Papadopoli. You step straight into the original palace, with stuccoed rooms and the addition of a small spa and a gym. The hotel has spacious common rooms and lovely gardens.

Bauer Palazzo

MAP P5 ■ Campo San Moisè, S Marco 1459 ■ 041 520 70 22 ■ www. bauerhotels.com ■ €€€
Close to St Mark's Square amid the main sights and best shops, the Bauer offers old-style service in swish surroundings.

Excelsior Venice Lido Resort

MAP H2 ■ Lungomare Marconi 41, Lido ■ 041 526 02 01 ■ www.hotel excelsiorvenezia.com ■ Closed Nov–mid-Mar ■ €€€
Crawling with stars during the Film Festival (see p62), this hotel has rooms right on the beach. There is also a swimming pool and exclusive restaurants.

Hotel Cipriani

MAP E6 ■ Giudecca 10 ■ 041 520 77 44 ■ www. hotelcipriani.com ■ Closed Nov–Mar ■ €€€
Set on Giudecca, Cipriani is just minutes from the water. It has a private garden with a salt-water pool, and three top restaurants (see p64).

Hotel Danieli

MAP R5 ■ Riva degli Schiavoni, Castello 4196 ■ 041 522 64 80 ■ www. danielihotelvenice.com ■ €€€
Set in a pink palazzo, Danieli has a long history of famous guests (see p109). The hotel is close to the Bridge of Sighs and Piazza San Marco.

JW Marriott Venice Resort

MAP N4 ■ Isole delle Rose, Venice Lagoon ■ 041 296 81 11 ■ www.jwvenice. com ■ Closed Nov–Feb ■ Disabled access ■ €€€
In parkland on an island in the Southern Lagoon, this resort offers suites, roof terraces, swimming pools, a spa and a choice of restaurants. Daily cooking classes on offer. Private shuttle launch takes 20 minutes to reach Piazza San Marco.

Luna Hotel Baglioni

MAP P5 ■ Calle Larga dell'Ascension, S Marco 1243 ■ 041 528 98 40 ■ www.baglionihotels. com ■ €€€
Exquisite service in a sophisticated atmosphere of chandeliers and marble. This is Venice's oldest hotel, and it hosted Knights Templar in the 1100s, while they waited to embark for the Crusades. Breakfast is served in the drawing room, frescoed by pupils of Tiepolo (see p48).

Metropole

MAP F4 ■ Riva degli Schiavoni, Castello 4149 ■ 041 520 50 44 ■ www. hotelmetropole.com ■ €€€
This is a majestic good-value establishment, immaculately run. On the waterfront, minutes from San Marco, it boasts a wonderful garden and a Michelin-starred restaurant.

Palace Bonvecchiati

MAP Q4 ■ Calle dei Fabbri, S Marco 4680 ■ 041 296 31 11 ■ www.palace bonvecchiati.it ■ €€€
"Contemporary luxury" best describes this hotel with a roof-level sauna and gym. Private canal access means guests can arrive by water taxi.

The Westin Europa & Regina
MAP P6 ▪ Corte Barozzi, S Marco 2159 ▪ 041 240 00 01 ▪ www.westin europareginavenice.com ▪ Disabled access ▪ €€€
This elegant historic palace, on the Grand Canal, is beautifully decorated. It is also quite close to the Piazza San Marco.

Budget Hotels

Al Campaniel Guesthouse
MAP L4 ▪ Calle del Campaniel, S Polo 2889 ▪ 041 275 07 49 ▪ www. alcampaniel.com ▪ No disabled access ▪ €
Spanish-Venetian couple Gloria and Marco are discreet and professional hosts who offer spotless rooms close to the San Tomà boat stop. Each room has tea- and coffee-making facilities.

Al Santo
Via del Santo 147, Padua ▪ 049 875 21 31 ▪ Closed 7–30 Jan ▪ www.alsanto.it ▪ €
This simple hotel is very well located, 10 minutes' stroll from Padua's main sights (see p129).

Alloggi Gerotto Calderan
MAP C2 ▪ Campo S Geremia, Cannaregio 283 ▪ 041 715 361 ▪ Closed Christmas week ▪ www. casagerottocalderan.com ▪ No credit cards ▪ No disabled access ▪ €
Handy for the station, with airy rooms, some with bath (no breakfast). Guests are welcomed by enthusiastic English-speaking staff. Try to bargain down the rates in low season.

Bernardi Semenzato
MAP P1 ▪ Calle dell'Oca, Cannaregio 4366 ▪ 041 522 72 57 ▪ www.hotel bernardi.com ▪ Limited disabled access ▪ €
Located near Campo dei Santi Apostoli, this hotel is a delightful bargain. The owners are extremely hospitable.

Casa Cardinal Piazza
MAP D1 ▪ Fondamenta Contarini, Cannaregio 3539/A ▪ 041 721 388 ▪ www.casacardinal piazza.org ▪ No credit cards ▪ No air conditioning ▪ No disabled access ▪ €
Great-value palace guest-house run by friendly nuns and set in a shady garden right on the lagoon edge. Breakfast available; 11pm curfew.

Hotel Gobbo
MAP C2 ▪ Campo S Geremia 312, Cannaregio ▪ 041 715 001 ▪ www. albergoalgobbo.it ▪ No disabled access ▪ €
The "Hunchback" is a clean, small-scale hotel. Most of the rooms have air conditioning, and a couple overlook a bustling square. Easy access from the railway station.

Istituto Canossiano
MAP K6 ▪ Fondamenta delle Eremite, Dorsoduro 1323 ▪ 041 240 97 13 ▪ Closed Christmas week, 2 weeks in Aug ▪ www. romite1323.com ▪ No air conditioning ▪ No disabled access ▪ €
A modernized, converted convent with vast court-yards to wander around. Vending machines are on hand for snacks and drinks; otherwise, it's not far to the Zattere. There's a midnight curfew.

Il Lato Azzurro
MAP H2 ▪ Via Forti 13, Sant'Erasmo ▪ 041 523 06 42 ▪ www.latoazzurro.it ▪ No air conditioning ▪ Limited disabled access ▪ €
Great-value lodgings on this garden island, where sea breezes are ensured. The hosts can arrange canoe trips, bicycles, picnic lunches and half-board, entailing mainly vegetarian meals. The hotel has two rooms specially equipped for disabled travellers.

San Giorgio Monastery
MAP F5 ▪ Isola di San Giorgio Maggiore ▪ 041 241 47 17 ▪ No credit cards ▪ €
The monks on San Giorgio Island, just across the Canale di San Marco from Piazza San Marco, welcome guests to their peaceful premises. A simple breakfast is provided, and self-catering accommodation is also available. There are superb views of Venice from the square in front of the church.

Hotels with Charm

Ca' del Borgo
MAP F1 ▪ Piazza delle Erbe 8, Malamocco ▪ 041 770 749 ▪ www. cadelborgo.com ▪ €
This charming 14th-century villa is located on the southern end of the Lido, in an old fishing village. The Ca' del Moro Sporting Club has a swimming pool, tennis and physical fitness facilities There is easy access to Venice and the beach.

Accademia Villa Maravege
MAP L6 ▪ Fondamenta Bollani, Dorsoduro 1058 ▪ 041 521 01 88 ▪ www.pensioneaccademia.it ▪ Limited disabled access ▪ €€–€€€

This beautiful 17th-century villa near the Accademia *(see pp30–31)* was formerly the Russian embassy. Breakfast can be enjoyed in the private garden. You need to book well in advance.

Ca' della Corte
MAP B3 ▪ Corte Surian, Dorsoduro 3560 ▪ 041 715 877 ▪ www.cadellacorte.com ▪ No disabled access ▪ €€

Charming bed-and-breakfast with spotless rooms that boast all the latest equipment, including satellite TV. Very handy to Piazzale Roma.

La Calcina
MAP D5 ▪ Zattere, Dorsoduro 780 ▪ 041 520 64 66 ▪ www.lacalcina.com ▪ No disabled access ▪ €€

In 1877, Ruskin stayed at this guesthouse on the Zattere. The rooms have been modernized since then, but they retain their charm and parquet floors. An exclusive street-level terrace overlooks the Giudecca Canal, while another surveys the roof-tops. It is advised to book in advance for a stay here.

Hotel Flora
MAP P5 ▪ Calle Bergamaschi, S Marco 2283/A ▪ 041 520 58 44 ▪ www.hotelflora.it ▪ No disabled access ▪ €€

Though small, the pretty courtyard here with lush greenery is an oasis of calm after the city crowds. Good views from the upper rooms.

Hotel Marconi
MAP P3 ▪ Riva del Vin, S Polo 729 ▪ 041 522 20 68 ▪ www.hotelmarconi.it ▪ No disabled access ▪ €€

Popular hotel by Rialto Bridge, with outside seating reserved for guests. Warm reception but simple rooms.

Locanda Cipriani
MAP H1 ▪ Piazza S Fosca 29, Torcello ▪ 041 730 150 ▪ www.locandacipriani.com ▪ No disabled access ▪ Closed Jan–early Feb ▪ €€

A peaceful, sophisticated place on the island of Torcello *(see pp36–7)*, with a list of illustrious past guests, and a famed restaurant overlooking the garden. Guests can explore the island after the day-trippers have left.

Palazzo Abadessa
MAP D2 ▪ Calle Priuli, Cannaregio 4011 ▪ 041 241 37 84 ▪ www.abadessa.com ▪ Limited disabled access ▪ €€–€€€

Murano glass chandeliers and lovely fabrics add to the authentic atmosphere at this palace hotel. Two specially equipped rooms for disabled travellers.

San Simon Ai Due Fanali
MAP K1 ▪ Campo S Simeone Grande, S Croce 946/949 ▪ 041 718 490 ▪ www.aiduefanali.com ▪ No disabled access ▪ €€

The rooms at this tastefully renovated former monastery have wooden rafters. Several apartments are available near the Arsenale.

The Gritti Palace
MAP N6 ▪ Campo S Maria del Giglio, S Marco 2467 ▪ 041 794 611 ▪ www.thegrittipalace.com ▪ €€€

Ernest Hemingway stayed in this 15th-century palace-hotel situated on the Grand Canal. Romantic waterside dining is among its many features.

Converted Palaces

Albergo Guerrato
MAP N2 ▪ Calle Drio la Scimia, S Polo 240/A ▪ 041 528 59 27 ▪ Closed 7–30 Jan ▪ www.pensioneguerrato.it ▪ Not all rooms are en suite ▪ No disabled access ▪ €

This charming, spacious old place at Rialto dates back to 1288 and is full of history.

Al Sole
MAP J4 ▪ Fondamenta Minotto, S Croce 136 ▪ 041 244 03 28 ▪ www.alsolehotels.com ▪ No disabled access ▪ €€

A beautiful place to stay, convenient for Piazzale Roma, this 16th-century palace, with a huge lobby and a courtyard draped in wisteria, is often used as a film set. Rooms have all mod cons.

Ca' Nigra Lagoon Resort
MAP K1 ▪ Campo S Simeon Grande, S Croce 927 ▪ 041 275 00 47 ▪ www.hotelcanigra.com ▪ €€–€€€

Once an ambassador's residence, this palace on the Grand Canal has two delightful shady gardens. The decor is modern, and one room even has a private jacuzzi. The location is handy for the railway and bus stations.

Ca' Pisani

MAP F4 ■ Rio Terrà Foscarini, Dorsoduro 979A ■ 041 240 14 11 ■ www.capisanihotel.it ■ Limited disabled access ■ €€

Converted in 2000, Ca' Pisani has a warm ambience, stunning modern design and all the facilities you could hope for. You may never want to leave this 15th-century palace, conveniently close to the Accademia.

Hotel Santo Stefano

MAP M5 ■ Campo S Stefano, S Marco 2957 ■ 041 520 01 66 ■ www. hotelsantostefano venezia.com ■ No disabled access ■ €€

Guests return to this former monastery watchtower for the discerning style, maximum comfort (Jacuzzis in all rooms) and breathtaking views.

Locanda La Corte

MAP F3 ■ Calle Bressana, Castello 6317 ■ 041 241 13 00 ■ www.locanda lacorte.it ■ No disabled access ■ €€

A relaxing atmosphere prevails at this renovated 16th-century palace. It once served the ambassador from Brescia and is impeccably furnished with period pieces. Breakfast is served in the courtyard.

Locanda San Barnaba

MAP L5 ■ Calle del Traghetto, Dorsoduro 2785–2786 ■ 041 241 12 33 ■ www.locanda-san barnaba.com ■ Limited disabled access ■ €€

Minutes from the Ca' Rezzonico ferry stop, this quiet, elegant palace-hotel has original frescoes in many of the rooms, which are named after Goldoni's plays.

San Cassiano – Ca' Favretto

MAP N2 ■ Calle della Rosa, S Croce 2232 ■ 041 524 17 68 ■ www. sancassiano.it ■ €€

Right on the Grand Canal, but hidden in the maze of alleyways close to Rialto, you'll find this 16th-century palace converted into a hotel named after a 19th-century artist. Elegant, well-equipped rooms.

Ruzzini Palace Hotel

MAP R3 ■ Campo S Maria Formosa, Castello 5866 ■ 041 241 04 47 ■ www.ruzzinipalace.com ■ €€€

Constructed in the late 16th century, this period residence retains its vast frescoed rooms, monumental staircases and a water entrance. It overlooks a typical Venetian square and is only five minutes from Piazza San Marco.

Hotels in Tranquil Locations

Agriturismo Le Garzette

MAP H2 ■ Lungomare Alberoni 32, Malamocco, Lido ■ 041 731 078 ■ Closed Christmas–Feb ■ www.legarzette.it ■ No disabled access ■ €

This attractive family-run establishment, off the beaten track, has only five rooms and this – along with the superb home cooking – will make you feel as though you are part of the family. Close to the sea and the lagoon.

Ca' San Marcuola

MAP C2 ■ Campiello della Chiesa, Cannaregio 1763 ■ 041 716 048 ■ Closed Dec–Carnival ■ www. casanmarcuola.com ■ Disabled access ■ €

In a handy location close to the *vaporetto* stop, this unpretentious, but quiet and friendly, guesthouse is well appointed.

Due Mori

Contrà Do Rode 24–26, Vicenza ■ 044 432 18 86 ■ Closed 1–15 Aug ■ www.hotelduemori. com ■ Disabled access ■ No air conditioning ■ €

In a quiet street in Vicenza, close to all the main sights *(see p130)*, the Due Mori has spacious, spotless rooms furnished in old-style dark timber.

Villa Ducale

Riviera Martiri della Libertà 75, Dolo ■ ACTV bus 53 from Piazzale Roma ■ 041 560 80 20 ■ www.villaducale.it ■ Limited disabled access ■ €

Halfway between Padua and Venice, this stately residence stands in a lovely private park with statues. The beautiful rooms have the usual facilities plus frescoes and glass chandeliers.

Ca' Vendramin di Santa Fosca

MAP D2 ■ Fondamenta Vendramin, Cannaregio 2400 ■ 041 275 0125 ■ www.hotelcaven dramin.it ■ Limited disabled access ■ €€

The comfortable rooms in this cosy 16th-century palazzo just off the Strada Nova are lavishly decorated. Breakfast is served in a period-style room.

Dell'Alboro

MAP M4 ■ Corte dell'Alboro, S Marco 3894/A-B ■ 041 522 94 54 ■ Closed 20 Nov–20 Dec ■ www.alborohotel.it ■ No disabled access ■ €€
Located in a relaxing residential area near the Sant'Angelo boat stop, this hotel has rooms with all modern facilities and is centrally located for Piazza San Marco.

Hotel Falier

MAP K4 ■ Salizzada S Pantalon, S Croce 130 ■ 041 710 882 ■ www. hotelfalier.com ■ Limited disabled access ■ €€
This cheery place is named after the beheaded traitor Doge Falier, "as a warning to guests who fail to pay!" Sunlight streams into the comfortable, if small, rooms, all of them with a shower. There's a court-yard dripping with wisteria.

Locanda Fiorita

MAP M5 ■ Campiello Novo o dei Morti, S Marco 3457/A ■ 041 523 47 54 ■ www.locandafiorita.com ■ No disabled access ■ €€
A very pretty place on a sunny square that was once a public cemetery, off Campo San Stefano. In spring and summer, enjoy a leisurely breakfast out-side. Bargain for cheaper rooms in low season.

Bauer Palladio

MAP E6 ■ Giudecca 33 ■ 041 520 70 22 ■ Closed mid-Nov–Mar ■ www. palladiohotelspa.com ■ €€€
This exclusive spa hotel was originally designed in the 1500s by Palladio as an orphanage. It has an array of facilities, a vast garden and a restaurant.

Medium-Priced Hotels

Al Gallion

MAP K2 ■ Calle Gallion, S Croce 1126 ■ 041 524 47 43 ■ www.algallion. com ■ No disabled access ■ No credit cards ■ No air conditioning ■ €
Guests are given a warm welcome and insider infor-mation at this small B&B. It is handy for Piazzale Roma and the Riva di Biasio vaporetto stop on the Grand Canal.

Al Saor

MAP P1 ■ Calle Zotti, Cannaregio 3904/A ■ 041 296 06 54 ■ www.alsaor.com ■ No disabled access ■ €
The owners of this family-run establishment, close to the Ca' d'Oro, offer personal touches: a ride in their own boat for guests, and home-made biscuits for breakfast.

Hotel Torcolo

Vicolo Listone 3, Verona ■ Bus Nos. 11, 12, 13, 51 (or 90, 92, 93 evenings & hols) from Marciapiede A ■ 045 800 75 12 ■ Closed Christmas week ■ www. hoteltorcolo.it ■ No disabled access ■ €
Just around the corner from the Arena, the hotel is run by a very friendly team. Guest parking available.

Locanda Ca' Zose

MAP D5 ■ Calle del Bastion, Dorsoduro 193/B ■ 041 522 66 35 ■ www. hotelcazose.com ■ No disabled access ■ €–€€
Cosy, immaculate rooms, several with canal views. Very quiet, handy for La Salute vaporetto and the Guggenheim.

Rossi

MAP C2 ■ Calle Procuratie, Cannaregio 262 ■ 041 715 164 ■ Closed 6 Jan–6 Feb ■ www.hotelrossi.ve.it ■ No disabled access ■ €
Recommended family hotel, high on hospitality. Spotless rooms, many with lovely views. The hotel is well placed for Strada Nova. Book in advance.

Villa Giustinian

Via Miranese 85, Mirano ■ 041 570 02 00 ■ www. villagiustinian.com ■ Disabled access ■ €
An 18th-century villa with a swimming pool, park, magnificent rooms and a fine restaurant. Buses every 20 minutes for the 40-minute trip to Venice.

Al Gambero

MAP P4 ■ Calle dei Fabbri, S Marco 4687 ■ 041 522 43 84 ■ www. locandaalgambero.com ■ No disabled access ■ €€
This old favourite on a bridge halfway between Rialto and the Piazza San Marco is wonderful for many sights and shopping sprees. Downstairs is Le Bistrot, a popular nightspot (see p69).

Al Gazzettino

MAP Q4 ■ Calle di Mezzo, S Marco 4971 ■ 041 528 65 23 ■ www.algazzettino. com ■ No disabled access ■ €€
Centrally located between the Rialto and San Marco, Al Gazzettino is a basic, decent-value hotel. The downstairs walls are papered with sheets from the city's Il Gazzettino

newspaper, which was its long-standing neighbour until its relocation to the more practical mainland.

Hotel Novecento
MAP N6 ▪ Calle del Dose, Campo San Maurizio, San Marco 2683 ▪ 041 241 37 65 ▪ www.novecento.biz ▪ No disabled access ▪ €€
The relaxing rooms at this boutique hotel, located halfway between the Accademia and Piazza San Marco, are oriental in ambience. In summer, breakfast is served in the courtyard.

Hostels and Campsites

Campeggio Miramare
Lungomare D. Alighieri 29, Punta Sabbione ▪ 041 966 150 ▪ Closed Nov–late Mar ▪ www.camping-miramare.it ▪ €
One of the many camping grounds at Punta Sabbioni on the seaside of Venice, Miramare is linked to the city by ferry (line LN). The camping village has huts and campsites and also offers a range of facilities, including a mini-market and a restaurant-bar.

Camping Fusina
Via Moranzani 93, Fusina ▪ 041 547 00 55 ▪ www.camping-fusina.com ▪ €
Popular three-star venue for campers and back-packers (in a caravan), right on the lagoon edge. It is well connected via bus No. 11 from Mestre railway station or the Alilaguna ferry from the Zattere in Venice.

Foresteria Valdese
MAP R3 ▪ Calle Lunga S Maria Formosa, Castello 5170 ▪ 041 528 67 97 ▪ www.foresteria venezia.it ▪ €
A wonderful guesthouse near Campo Santa Maria Formosa (see p110), Palazzo Cavagnis is run by the Waldensian and Methodist community and has frescoed dormitories, and two, three and four-bed rooms. Be sure to book in advance.

IYH Città di Padova
Via Aleardo Aleardi 30, Padua ▪ Bus Nos. 8, 12 or tram from Padua railway station to Prato della Valle ▪ 049 875 22 19 ▪ Closed 22 Dec–6 Jan ▪ www.ostellopadova.it ▪ €
A bit out of the way, but only a short walk to the main sights, this hostel benefits from a beautiful setting in an ornamental grassy square.

IYH Ostello Olimpico
Viale Giuriolo 7, Vicenza ▪ Bus Nos. 2, 5 or 7 from the railway station ▪ 0444 540 222 ▪ Closed early Nov–Feb ▪ www.ostello vicenza.com ▪ €
A cheery, helpful hostel close to the main tourist office and Teatro Olimpico (see p131). Discounts apply at a neighbouring bar and restaurant. Internet point and bike hire available.

IYH Ostello Venezia
MAP E6 ▪ Fondamenta Zitelle 86, Giudecca ▪ 041 877 82 88 ▪ www.generatorhostels.com ▪ €
Well-run hostel offering cheap meals and a lovely setting on Giudecca, a 35-minute *vaporetto* trip from the railway station

(line No. 82) and five minutes to Piazza San Marco (see pp20–23).

IYH Ostello Villa Francescatti
Salita Fontana del Ferro 15, Verona ▪ Bus No. 73 (Mon–Sat), 91 (evenings & Sun) from the railway station ▪ 045 590 360 ▪ www.ostelloverona.it ▪ €
This 16th-century villa on the hillside above the Roman amphitheatre is also the official youth hostel, with dormitories. It is just 3 km (2 miles) from Verona's train station.

Ostello a Colori
Via Giare 169, Giare di Mira ▪ Venice–Chioggia bus line, Giare bus stop ▪ 0348 324 4832 ▪ Closed Oct–Feb ▪ www.ostello-acolori.org ▪ €
This hostel is located just outside Venice in a lovely country setting. Car parking is available. All linen is provided.

Ostello Santa Fosca
MAP D2 ▪ Fondamenta Canal, Cannaregio 2372 ▪ 041 715 775 ▪ www.ostellosantafosca.it ▪ €
University student hostel set in rambling convent grounds that lets out dorm beds to back-packers. Cooking facilities are available in summer.

Venezia Camping Village
MAP G1 ▪ Via Orlanda 8d, Mestre ▪ 041 531 28 28 ▪ Closed early Nov–Feb ▪ €
Popular site for campers and bungalow rentals. Verdant area, immaculate buildings and a pool. Bus Nos. 5 and 19 take you to Venice in 5 minutes.

Index

Acknowledgments

Author

Gillian Price was born in England in 1953 and grew up in Sydney, Australia. She moved to Venice in 1981 and has written nine books on walking in Italy. Gillian has been contributing to DK's Eyewitness Guides since 1998.

Additional contributor Kate Hughes

Publishing Director Georgina Dee

Publisher Vivien Antwi

Design Director Phil Ormerod

Editorial Parnika Bagla, Michelle Crane, Rebecca Flynn, Rachel Fox, Freddie Marriage, Fíodhna Ní Ghríofa, Scarlett O'Hara, Adrian Potts, Sally Schafer, Sands Publishing Solutions

Design Richard Czapnik, Sunita Gahir, Bharti Karakoti

Picture Research Susie Peachey, Ellen Root, Lucy Sienkowska, Oran Tarjan

Cartography Zafar ul Islam Khan, Suresh Kumar, Casper Morris

DTP Jason Little, George Nimmo, Azeem Siddiqui

Production Linda Dare

Factchecker Charles Hebbert

Proofreader Ruth Reisenberger

Indexer Helen Peters

Illustrator Chris Orr & Associates
First edition created by Book Creation Services Ltd, London

Commissioned Photography Demetrio Carrasco, John Heseltine, Anna Mockford, Roger Moss, William Reavell, Rough Guides/Michelle Grant, Rough Guides/James McConnachie, Rough Guides/Martin Richardson.

Picture Credits

The publisher would like to thank the following for their kind permission to reproduce their photographs.

Key: a-above; b-below/bottom; c-centre; f-far; l-left; r-right; t-top

4Corners: Luca Da Ros 4t.

Alamy Images: A.F. Archive 63tr; age fotostock/Jose Peral 59tl, 104br; AGF Srl/Mark Edward Smith 14bl; Alessandro0770 15b; The Art Archive/Collection Dagli Orti 19tl, 23cl; Peter Barritt 27b, 32cla; Bildarchiv Monheim GmbH 36bl; blickwinkel 109br; Paul Carstairs 82c; dpa picture alliance 111bl; Eye Ubiquitous/Paul Seheult 37ca; Peter Erik Forsberg 75cb; funkyfood, London/Paul Williams 10cra; Rik Hamilton 6cla; Hemis.fr / Christian Guy 117bl; Heritage Image Partnership Ltd 49cl, /Fine Art Images 18tl; John Heseltine 73cla; Peter Horree 48b; IML Image Group/Roberto Meazza 134bl; Interfoto 45bl, /Fine Arts 45tl; John Warburton-Lee Photography /Ken Scicluna 106clb; Rebecca Johnson 65bl; Konstantin Kalishko 23b; John Keats 14cra; John Kellerman 17cra, 38-9,

104cl; Alvan Kranzer 45tr; liszt collection/Quint & Lox 47bl; Dennis MacDonald 111cla; Martin Thomas Photography 114-5; Mary Evans Picture Library 44cb; Thomas Mayer 103tr; Moviestore Collection Ltd 47tr; Erick Nguyen 51bl; North Wind Picture Archives 44cla; Sergey Novikov 108ca; Chuck Pefley 35tl; peterforsberg 75cla; Ferdinando Piezzi 118tl; Prisma Archivo 46cr; Prisma Bildagentur AG/ Sonderegger Christof 57tl; Alex Ramsay 60t; Realy Easy Star/Giuseppe Masci 133bl; Reda & Co srl/Federico Meneghetti 129br; Matthias Scholz 49tr; Unlisted Images, Inc./ Fotosearch 38bl; Peter Vallance 57b; Martyn Vickery 34br; Visions of Serge L 119bl; Ross Warner 37tl, 59b; World History Archive 16cb, 48tl; Zoonar GmbH/Francesco Perre 39bc.

Arnoldo Battois: 84bc.

Bacarando: 86c.

Osteria Bancogiro: 93ca.

Bevilacqua Tessuti: 85crb.

Bistrot de Venise: 69b.

Signor Blum: 100clb.

Bragorà: 112bl.

Bridgeman Images: Cameraphoto Arte Venezia 19b.

Cesare Sent SNC: 120tc.

Corbis: Alinari Archives/Mauro Magliani 31clb; Atlantide Phototravel/Stefano Amantini 61cr; David Lees 31cla; Sylvain Sonnet 17cl; The Gallery Collection 15cl.

Dreamstime.com: Andreykr 34-5; Antonella865 37bc; Michal Bednarek 24-5; Briggsphoto 76cr; Canonman29 25cra, 82tr, 89tr; Carolannefreeling 50clb; Marco Clarizia 33tr; Richard Clarke 77br; Crisferra 56c; Dbdella 34clb; Razvan Ionut Dragomirescu 110cla; Viorel Dudau 46tl; Eg004713 128tl; Ekaterinabelova 18br, 123tl; Emicristea 13tr; Liliia Epifanova 77cl; Fedecandoniphoto 25br; Inna Felker 51tr; Michael Foley 53tr; Gekkon4ik 26crb; Ihsan Gercelman 6br; Radu Razvan Gheorghe 75tr; Diana Gradeva 116cla; Mark Graham 11cla; Neil Harrison 13cr; Anna Hristova 88cra; Lukasz Janyst 20-1; Wieslaw Jarek 10cl, 20br, 21bl; Jocrebbin 118bl; Johnnydevil 11br; Krontus 112c; Lachris77 2tr, 42-3; Lejoch 17tl, 50t; Ron Lima 4b; Lornet 10bl; Lucidwaters 71tr; Mapics 10-1b; Milosk50 32-3, 39tl; minnystock 2tl, 8-9; Evgeniya Moroz 12-3; NatashaBreen 36-7; Nikonaft 123br; Andrey Omelyanchuk 13clb; Carlos Sanchez Pereyra 118crb; Phant 4cla; Valeriya Potapova 94-5; Beatrice Preve 1; Rndmst 76tl; Sandyprints 73tr; Sborisov 24bl, 28-9; Jozef Sedmak 83bl, 99tl; Sindorei 109cra; Paula Stanley 74tl; Stevanzz 3tr, 7cl, 16c, 35b, 136-7; Stokkete 101tlc; Christophe Testi 98ca; Rachel Thomas 112tr; Giovanni Triggiani 27cla; VanderWolf Images 77cr; Christophe Villedieu 12clb; Niko Vukelic 3tl, 78-9; Tosca Weijers 130c; Oleg Znamenskiy 90bl, 96tl, 117cra.

Enoiteca Mascareta: 113cr.

Enoteca Do Colonne: 66br.

Fondazione Musei Civici di Venezia: Ca' Pesaro

– Galleria Internazionale d'Arte Moderna «November» 1870 by Telemaco Signorini 55bl; Ca' Rezzonico - Museo del Settecento Veneziano Scalone d'onore, (1753-1756) by Giorgio Massari 24br; Museo Correr 55tl, Mark Edward Smith 22bl, statue of Orfeo (1775 - 1776) Pietra di Vicenza by Antonio Canova photo Mark Edward Smith 22ca; Museo Storico Navale 55cr; Museo del Vetro, Murano Murano Glass, Compagnia Venezia Murano, 1878 54bc; Palazzo Ducale 16bl, 17c; Palazzo Fortuny/Courtesy Galleria Traghetto Venezia Shadows by Anne-Karin Furunes photo by Mark Edward Smith 83cla.

Fondazione Teatro La Fenice: MIchele Crosera 62tl, 62bl, 81br.

Getty Images: DEA/Dagli Orti 46bc, /F. Ferruzzi 11tl; DeAgostini 30-1, 33cr, 36cl; Fine Art Images / Heritage Images 30clb; Mondadori Portfolio 105cb; Picture Pos /Kurt Hutton 47cla; Mats Silvan 25tl.

Harry's Dolci: 127tr.

L'Isola - Carlo Moretti: 84cla.

La Caravella: 87crb.

La Pedrera: 92bl.

Luigi Bevilacqua: 70bl.

Madera: 100cr.

Palazzo Mocenigo: 90cra.

Muro Venezia S. Stae: 93tr.

Museo della Musica: 74br.

Museo di Storia Naturale: 60bc.

Palazzo Grassi S.p.A : Thomas Mayer 98br.

Peggy Guggenheim Collection: 40-1; Attirement of the Bride 1940 by Max Ernst © ADAGP, Paris and DACS, London 2016 40bl; Donna che cammina (Femme qui marche) (1936) © The Estate of Alberto Giacometti (Fondation Giacometti, Paris and ADAGP, Paris), licensed in the UK by ACS and DACS, London 2016 41tr.

Da Rioba: 107tr.

Ristorante Linea d'Ombre: 101cr.

Rizzo: 70cr.

Robert Harding Picture Library: age fotostock Doug Scott 72b; Dr. Wilfried Bahnmuller 20cl; Peter Barritt 24cla; Neil Emmerson 4cra, 21tl; Lee Frost 4clb; Sabine Lubenow 11cra, 34cla; Harrison Neil 21crb; Massimo Pizzotti 11tr; Roy Rainford 4cl; Tetra Images 4crb, 18c; Guy Thouvenin 11crb.

Studio Codex Venetia: 106tr.

Teatro Fondamenta Nuove: 63clb.

Tragicomica: 92cl.

Trattoria Alla Maddalena: 121cra.

Venetia Studium: 85tc.

Venturini Souvenirs: 126crb.

Cover
Front and spine - **Alamy Images:** Jan Wlodarczyk. Back - Dreamstime.com: Robyn Mackenzie.

Pull Out Map Cover
Alamy Images: Jan Wlodarczyk.

All other images are: © Dorling Kindersley. For further information see www.dkimages. com.

As a guide to abbreviations in visitor information blocks: **Adm** *= admission charge;* **DA** *= disabled access;* **D** *= dinner;* **L** *= lunch.*

Penguin
Random
House

Printed and bound in China

First published in Great Britain in 2002 by Dorling Kindersley Limited 80 Strand, London WC2R 0RL

Copyright 2002, 2016 © Dorling Kindersley Limited

A Penguin Random House Company

16 17 18 19 20 10 9 8 7 6 5 4 3 2 1

Reprinted with revisions 2003, 2005, 2007, 2009, 2011, 2013, 2015, 2016

A CIP catalogue record is available from the British Library.

ISBN 978 0 2412 0343 9

MIX
Paper from
responsible sources
FSC™ C018179
www.fsc.org

SPECIAL EDITIONS OF DK TRAVEL GUIDES

Phrase Book

In an Emergency

Help!	Aiuto!	eye-yoo-toh
Stop!	Fermate!	fair-mah-teh
Call a doctor.	Chiama un medico	kee-ah-mah oon meh-dee-koh
Call an ambulance.	Chiama un' ambulanza	kee-ah-mah oon am-boo-lan-tsa
Call the police.	Chiama la polizia	kee-ah-mah lah pol-ee-tsee-ah
Call the fire brigade.	Chiama i pompieri	kee-ah-mah ee pom-pee-air-ee

Communication Essentials

Yes/No	Sì/No	see/noh
Please	Per favore	pair fah-vor-eh
Thank you	Grazie	grah-tsee-eh
Excuse me	Mi scusi	mee skoo-zee
Hello	Buon giorno	bwon jor-noh
Goodbye	Arrivederci	ah-ree-veh-dair-chee
Good evening	Buona sera	bwon-ah sair-ah
What?	Quale?	kwah-leh?
When?	Quando?	kwan-doh?
Why?	Perchè?	pair-keh?
Where?	Dove?	doh-veh?

Useful Phrases

How are you?	Come sta?	koh-meh stah?
Very well, thank you.	Molto bene, grazie.	moll-toh beh-neh grah-tsee-eh
Pleased to meet you.	Piacere di conoscerla.	pee-ah-chair-eh dee-koh-noh-shair-lah
That's fine.	Va bene.	va beh-neh
Where is/are …?	Dov'è/Dove sono …?	dov-eh/doveh soh-noh …?
How do I get to …?	Come faccio per arrivare a …?	koh-meh fah choh pair arri-var-eh ah …?
Do you speak English?	Parla inglese?	par-lah een-gleh-zeh?
I don't understand.	Non capisco.	non ka-pee-skoh
I'm sorry.	Mi dispiace.	mee dee-spee-ah-cheh

Shopping

How much does this cost?	Quant'è, per favore?	kwan-teh pair fah-vor-eh?
I would like …	Vorrei …	vor-ray
Do you have …?	Avete …?	ah-veh-teh …?
Do you take credit cards?	Accettate carte di credito?	ah-chet-tah-teh kar-teh dee creh-dee-toh?
What time do you open/ close?	A che ora apre/ chiude?	ah keh or-ah ah-preh/ kee-oo-deh?
this one	questo	kweh-stoh
that one	quello	kwell-oh
expensive	caro	kar-oh
cheap	a buon prezzo	ah bwon pret-soh
size, clothes	la taglia	lah tah-lee-ah
size, shoes	il numero	eel noo-mair-oh
white	bianco	bee-ang-koh
black	nero	neh-roh
red	rosso	ross-oh
yellow	giallo	jal-loh
green	verde	vair-deh
blue	blu	bloo

Types of Shop

bakery	il forno /il panificio	eel forn-oh /eel pan-ee-fee-choh
bank	la banca	lah bang-kah
bookshop	la libreria	lah lee-breh-ree-ah
cake shop	la pasticceria	lah pas-tee-chair-ee-ah
chemist	la farmacia	lah far-mah-chee-ah
delicatessen	la salumeria	sah sah-loo-meh-ree-ah
department store	il grande magazzino	eel gran-deh mag-gad-zee-noh
grocery	la drogheria	lah droh-geh-ree-ah
hairdresser	il parrucchiere	eel par-oo-kee-air-eh
ice cream parlour	la gelateria	lah jel-lah-tair-ree-ah
market	il mercato	eel mair-kah-toh
newsstand	l'edicola	leh-dee-koh-lah
post office	l'ufficio postale	loo-fee-choh pos-tah-leh
supermarket	il supermercato	eel su-pair-mair-kah-toh
tobacconist	il tabaccaio	eel tah-bak-eye-oh
travel agency	l'agenzia di viaggi	lah-jen-tsee-ah dee vee-ad-jee

Sightseeing

art gallery	la pinacoteca	lah peena-koh-teh-kah
bus stop	la fermata dell'autobus	lah fair-mah-tah dell ow-toh-booss
church	la chiesa/ la basilica	lah kee-eh-zah lah ah-seel-i-kah
closed for holidays	chiuso per le ferie	kee-oo-zoh pair leh fair-ee-eh
garden	il giardino	eel jar-dee-no
museum	il museo	eel moo-zeh-oh
railway station	la stazione	lah stah-tsee-oh-neh
tourist information	l'ufficio di turismo	loo-fee-choh dee too-ree-smoh

Staying in a Hotel

Do you have any vacant rooms?	Avete camere libere?	ah-veh-teh kah-mair-eh lee bair-eh?
double room	una camera doppia	oona kah-mair-ah doh-pee-ah
with double bed	con letto matrimoniale	kon let-toh mah-tree-moh-nee-ah-leh
twin room	una camera con due letti	oona kah-mair ah kon doo-eh let-tee
single room	una camera singola	oona kah-mair-ah sing-goh-lah
room with a bath, shower	una camera con bagno, con doccia	oona kah-mair ah kon ban-yoh, kon dot-chah
I have a reservation.	Ho fatto una prenotazione.	oh fat-toh oona preh-noh-tah-tsee-oh-neh

Eating Out

Have you got a table for …?	Avete una tavola per …?	ah-veh-teh oona tah-voh-lah pair …?
I'd like to reserve a table.	Vorrei prenotare una tavola.	vor-ray preh-noh-tar-reh oona tah-voh-lah
breakfast	colazione	koh-lah-tsee-oh-neh
lunch	pranzo	pran-tsoh
dinner	cena	cheh-nah
the bill	il conto	eel kon-toh
waitress	cameriera	kah-mair-ee-air-ah
waiter	cameriere	kah-mair-ee-air-eh
fixed price menu	il menù a prezzo fisso	eel meh-noo ah pret-soh fee-soh
dish of the day	piatto del giorno	pee-ah-toh dell jor-no
starter	antipasto	an-tee-pass-toh
first course	il primo	eel pree-moh
main course	il secondo	eel seh-kon-doh
vegetables	i contorni	ee kon-tor-noh
dessert	il dolce	eel doll-cheh
cover charge	il coperto	eel koh-pair-toh
wine list	la lista dei vini	lah lee-stah day vee-nee
glass	il bicchiere	eel bee-kee-air-eh
bottle	la bottiglia	lah bot-teel-yah
knife	il coltello	eel kol-tell-oh
fork	la forchetta	lah for-ket-tah
spoon	il cucchiaio	eel koo-kee-eye-oh

Menu Decoder

l'acqua minerale	lah-kwah mee-nair-ah-leh	mineral water
gassata/ naturale	gah-zah-tah/ nah-too-rah-leh	fizzy/ still
agnello	ah-niell-oh	lamb
aglio	al-ee-oh	garlic
al forno	al for-noh	baked
alla griglia	ah-lah greel-yah	grilled
la birra	lah beer-rah	beer
la bistecca	lah bee-stek-kah	steak
il burro	eel boor-oh	butter
il caffè	eel kah-feh	coffee
la carne	la kar-neh	meat
carne di maiale	kar-neh dee mah-yah-leh	pork
la cipolla	la chip-oh-lah	onion
fagioli	ee fah-joh-lee	beans
il formaggio	eel for-mad-joh	cheese
le fragole	leh frah-goh-leh	strawberries
fritto misto	eel free-toh mees-toh	mixed fried fish
la frutta	la froot-tah	fruit
frutti di mare	froo-tee dee mah-reh	seafood
funghi	ee foon-ghee	mushrooms
gamberi	ee gam-bair-ee	prawns
gelato	jel-lah-toh	ice cream
insalata	een-sah-lah-tah	salad
latte	eel laht-teh	milk
manzo	eel man-tsoh	beef
olio	eel oh-lee-oh	oil
pane	eel pah-neh	bread
le patate	leh pah-tah-teh	potatoes
le patatine fritte	leh pah-tah-teen-eh free-teh	chips
il pepe	eel peh-peh	pepper
il pesce	eel pesh-eh	fish
il pollo	eel poll-oh	chicken
il pomodoro	eel poh-moh-dor-oh	tomato
il prosciutto cotto/crudo	eel pro-shoo-toh kot-toh/ kroo-doh	ham cooked/cured
il riso	eel ree-zoh	rice
il sale	eel sah-leh	salt
la salsiccia	lah sal-see-chah	sausage
succo d'arancia/ di limone	soo-koh dah-ran-chah/ dee lee-moh-neh	orange/lemon juice
il tè	eel teh	tea
la torta	lah tor-tah	cake/tart
l'uovo	loo-oh-voh	egg
vino bianco	vee-noh bee-ang-koh	white wine
vino rosso	vee-noh ross-oh	red wine
le vongole	leh von-goh-leh	clams
lo zucchero	loh zoo-kair-oh	sugar
la zuppa	lah tsoo-pah	soup

Numbers

1	uno	oo-noh
2	due	doo-eh
3	tre	treh
4	quattro	kwat-roh
5	cinque	ching-kweh
6	sei	say-ee
7	sette	set-teh
8	otto	ot-toh
9	nove	noh-veh
10	dieci	dee-eh-chee
11	undici	oon-dee-chee
12	dodici	doh-dee-chee
13	tredici	tray-dee-chee
14	quattordici	kwat-tor-dee-chee
15	quindici	kwin-dee-chee
16	sedici	say-dee-chee
17	diciassette	dee-chah-set-teh
18	diciotto	dee-chot-toh
19	diciannove	dee-chah-noh-veh
20	venti	ven-tee
30	trenta	tren-tah
40	quaranta	kwah-ran-tah
50	cinquanta	ching-kwan-tah
60	sessanta	sess-an-tah
70	settanta	set-tan-tah
80	ottanta	ot-tan-tah
90	novanta	noh-van-tah
100	cento	chen-toh
1,000	mille	mee-leh
2,000	duemila	doo-eh mee-lah
1,000,000	un milione	oon meel-yoh-neh

Time

one minute	un minuto	oon mee-noo-toh
one hour	un'ora	oon or-ah
a day	un giorno	oon jor-noh
Monday	lunedì	loo-neh-dee
Tuesday	martedì	mar-teh-dee
Wednesday	mercoledì	mair-koh-leh-dee
Thursday	giovedì	joh-veh-dee
Friday	venerdì	ven-air-dee
Saturday	sabato	sah-bah-toh
Sunday	domenica	doh-meh-nee-kah

Index of Main Streets